PRAISE FOR *MEN'S WORK*

"Every now and then I come across a book that triggers a voice in my head that proclaims, 'Damn, I wish I had written this—this is really good.' My book-envy short list just grew by one more title: Men's Work. With this watershed book, Connor Beaton accomplishes the Herculean task—advanced by the forefathers of the modern men's movement: Carl Jung, Joseph Campbell, and Robert Bly—of creating an actionable game plan for alchemizing men's confusion, anger, and general male stupidity into purpose, healing, and mastery. From the Introduction on, Men's Work grabbed me by the mind, heart, and balls, and didn't let go. I am grateful to call Connor a friend, and I am even more grateful for the immeasurable gift he has given men and mankind with this book."

DR. ROBERT GLOVER
author of ***No More Mr. Nice Guy***

"Having known and worked with Connor throughout his journey, I can unequivocally say that this is the book every man needs. Connor does a beautiful job of inviting and leading us through our pain and back into our hearts. He reminds us that our darkness is to be embraced, not avoided."

MARK GROVES
human connection specialist
and founder of Create The Love

"In *Men's Work*, Connor Beaton eloquently illuminates the path for men to find deep healing and true freedom in their lives. A heavy burden is placed on men in our culture, and without guidance, they often suffer in silence. Connor is an incredible teacher and true alchemist—taking his own pain, sitting with it, and lovingly pouring the wisdom he gained from his own personal journey into this book so that others do the same. *Men's Work* is a hero's journey that I highly recommend to anyone looking to create a more peaceful, fulfilled life of purpose."

DR. NICOLE LEPERA
New York Times bestselling author
of ***How to Do the Work***

"Connor Beaton is truly one of the most valuable voices on comprehensive manhood today. His passionate but straightforward approach brilliantly unearths the excuses and vices that inhibit broken men from becoming whole. *Men's Work* is a powerful guide that will help men introspectively navigate to the healing they desire and deserve."

JASON WILSON
author of ***Cry Like a Man***

MEN'S WORK

A PRACTICAL GUIDE

TO FACE YOUR DARKNESS, END SELF-SABOTAGE, AND FIND FREEDOM

CONNOR BEATON

Sounds True
Boulder, CO 80306

Published 2023

Book design by Charli Barnes

Printed in Canada

BK06518

Library of Congress Cataloging-in-Publication Data

Names: Beaton, Connor, author.
Title: Men's work : a practical guide to face your darkness, end self-sabotage, and find freedom / by Connor Beaton.
Description: Boulder, CO : Sounds True, 2023. | Includes bibliographical references.
Identifiers: LCCN 2022040399 (print) | LCCN 2022040400 (ebook) | ISBN 9781683649908 (hardback) | ISBN 9781683649915 (ebook)
Subjects: LCSH: Self-actualization (Psychology) | Self-acceptance. | Masculinity. | Affirmations. | Interpersonal relations.
Classification: LCC BF637.S4 B39529 2023 (print) | LCC BF637.S4 (ebook) | DDC 158.1--dc23/eng/20220921
LC record available at https://lccn.loc.gov/2022040399
LC ebook record available at https://lccn.loc.gov/2022040400

10 9 8 7 6 5 4 3 2 1

For my two favorite stubborn hearts:
my wife, Vienna, and my son, Code.
You are the light guiding me on my path.

CONTENTS

PREFACE

BEFORE YOU BEGIN this journey, I thought it necessary to make a few things clear.

First, this is not my attempt to tell you what masculinity is, or how you should be as a man—although you may gain deep clarity about your own answers to these questions because of this work.

Second, over the past few decades, people have been talking about broken men, toxic masculinity, the crisis of masculinity, and countless other conversations all implying that men, collectively, have gone astray or are broken. Men are asked to change, be better, and heal with little to no direction outside of "be more vulnerable."

After years of my own development and nearly a decade of working with a multitude of men from around the globe, I began to see that there is a certain kind of intensity that lives within men that we have largely forgotten how to navigate. An intensity of pain, confusion, rage, fear, and grief that so many men carry but have not been shown how to integrate and leverage for our benefit and the benefit of the collective. An intensity that society largely rejects, ignores, or doesn't want to deal with, and that we as men have forgotten how to carry.

That is the aim of this book. To bring you into contact with your own intensity and pain so you can work with it. To help you learn—regardless of your faith, sexual orientation, or ethnicity—how to heal and be with the intensity of your own experience as a man.

I also want to emphasize that there are countless forms, versions, and aspects to men's work and that this is only one part of it. I don't claim to speak for all men doing this kind of work and am not so ignorant as to pretend like this is the only path. What follows is the work I had to engage in and the work I have brought countless men through. It is meant to be a guide for you as a man to step into your power through the door of healing.

Lastly, while I have tried to include as many experiences as humanly possible, I am sure I have left many out. While this book is unapologetically for men and is often geared toward male-female relationships, I try, where applicable, to include a range of sexual orientations. After working with men from countless walks of life, my intention is always to be as comprehensive as possible. If you find yourself feeling excluded, my suggestion is to move away from focusing on the external details of one man's story or background and return to the internal dynamics that connect us all.

INTRODUCTION

A MAN'S PATH TO FREEDOM

"There appears to be a conscience in mankind which severely punishes the man who does not somehow and at some time, at whatever cost to his pride, cease to defend and assert himself, and instead confess himself fallible and human."

CARL JUNG

THE WORK OF men begins with pain.

How are we as men to reconcile the sheer drive and determination we feel stirring in our souls with the intense confusion, anger, and emotional bleeding-out we can often feel?

Said more directly, how do we as men tune ourselves for something more than optimal performance in the boardroom or bedroom and overcome what stands in our way? How do we design within us a compass that can lead us through life's most violent storms? A compass that leads us toward depth—depth of experience, fulfillment, and purpose?

How do we as men develop *self-leadership*?

In order to do so, most men will, at some point, have to cross the threshold into the underworld of their own pain and come to grips with the following:

I am a man who has been abused.

I am a man who has abused others.

Or said another way:

I am a man who is hurting or has been hurt.

I am a man who has hurt others or is hurting others.

It took me decades to come to terms with these two statements, and they are now the driving force behind my life's work. Not because all men have been abused, or because these things define us as men, but because most men carry a pain within them they have never been taught to heal, work with, or use in a way that would give their life deeper meaning, direction, and purpose. But that's exactly what this book aims to accomplish.

To see the pain of men, you need not look far. Take a stroll around your workplace. Wander through your neighborhood. Talk to the men in your local bars, parks, and restaurants. Look into the eyes of the man sitting on the bus across from you, and behind his hard, protective exterior you'll see the neglected responsibilities, failed relationships, and a deep fear of being seen as an imposter. These men, at their core, do not feel in control of their hearts and minds.

Because a man who avoids his pain is a man who is enslaved by it.

This is the step-by-step doctrine men are taught for dealing with pain:

1) Suck it up.

2) Stuff it down.

3) Pour a bottle of whiskey over the top and finish it all off by rubbing one out for good measure.

4) Rinse (maybe) and repeat as necessary until sufficiently numbed out or forgotten about.

Unfortunately, this is the path so many men take. Hell, it's the path I walked for a long time. We trade internal leadership, liberty, and masculinity for a safe job, mediocre marriage, and a lifetime of unactioned dreams, all in the quest of pain avoidance. We feel lost, alone, incapable of change, and helpless against the daily onslaught of internal criticism, doubt, and worries.

We have, in many ways, been sold a lie; a lie of separation.

We have been indoctrinated into a cult; the cult of specialness.

And we have an amnesia to truth; the truth of *pain being a path to purpose.*

So how do we reconcile with the pain we've been given as men, or the pain we've caused? How do we make amends for the abuse, neglect, abandonment, and trauma we may have caused ourselves and others? Is there a way to alchemize the pain we carry into a purpose? Outside of the altruistic reasoning for embarking on this quest emerges the question most men ask repeatedly: "Why should I even bother?"

Because as Robert Bly, famous poet and father of the mythopoetic men's movement, famously said, "Where a man's wound is, that's where his genius will be."

STARTING FROM (ROCK) BOTTOM

I woke up in the back seat of my car as I had done every day for the past few weeks, shoulders aching and hips cramped from stuffing my six-foot-two frame into the back seat of my two-door Pontiac G5 coupe. Nothing beats a sunrise when you're viewing it from the parking lot of the local Walmart.

It was 2010 and I couldn't hide any longer. I'd spent years trying to ignore the man I'd become. For more than a decade I curated the facade of a man I thought people wanted me to be—the nice guy. The successful man with an exciting career that took him around the world. The guy with the perfect relationship, gorgeous girlfriend, motorcycle, and cars. Externally, I thought, I was the epitome of modern masculinity.

But the man I'd hidden could no longer be concealed. The lying man, the cheating man, the angry man, and the deeply isolated and lonely man had finally come out from behind the mask.

Leading up to my stay in chateau Walmart I had been in a downward spiral for years, but I had stuffed it deep down inside. Abusing alcohol, food, drugs, porn, and sex had come to an abrupt halt. I had been running full sprint away from my own darkness only to have it show up in front of me like a brick wall. More on the particulars of this later. For now, what you need to know is . . .

I knew I was the problem, but I didn't know how to escape, fix, or change anything.

Sound familiar?

I'd known for years I was out of control. I wasn't addicted to anything specific, aside from the constant need to make decisions that would leave me with crippling shame, anger, or guilt. Or perhaps I was addicted to gratification—trying to fill a space that was in truth an unfillable abyss. Watching porn for hours at a time most days, drinking entire bottles of Jack Daniel's or Southern Comfort as fast as I could, street racing motorcycles, running from the cops, and sleeping with as many women as possible all while maintaining full-time relationships and attempting to build a career as an opera singer (sounds like a terrible plotline from an eighties soap opera, I know).

Two weeks prior to the Walmart sunrise-through-my-windshield, my girlfriend caught me cheating. It wasn't the first time. It unfortunately wouldn't be the last time, but it was definitely the most devastating time.

This is normally where you'd get the salacious details about my escapades and read on wondering if you were consuming some poorly executed *Californication* reboot script, only to find out that the guy playing David Duchovny is far less charismatic and, for some strange reason, sings opera. But out of respect for those involved, who likely don't want their lives aired out like three-day-old underwear, I'll get to the point.

I felt out of control, and it finally caught up to me. I was a reactive man. A man who lacked self-leadership, self-compassion, and who loathed the idea of needing to admit his wrongs or ask for support.

I cheated on every woman I dated. I lied, manipulated, ran, and hid all my extracurricular activities from everyone in my life.

I was the worst kind of asshole—the kind who seemed like a genuinely good guy when you met him. I was "the Nice Guy," the classic wolf in sheep's clothing.

But that was the problem. No one knew. I was hiding the pain from my past, and I refused to admit all of the pain and destruction I was passing along to the people I loved. I had no men in my life challenging me.

No one calling me forward into my potential, no one to talk to about the deep pain I felt for the man I had become, and no one to help me clean up the mess of my life.

I felt helpless against the ever-raging inner critic, powerless to choose a different path, lost without a map or compass, and trapped with the overwhelming anger, grief, and sadness that I had carried from years of self-sabotage.

Up until that point, if you'd met me, you'd think I was doing great. But inside my head and heart, I felt out of control, lacked routines or direction, and had the kind of inner critic who would put the most abusive father in his place. This, I would later come to find, is the case with millions of men.

There, on day seventeen of sleeping in parking lots, avoiding calls from friends and family, showering at work, and swimming in a rising tide of fast-food wrappers, I reached a critical mass in my car. I cried myself to sleep more nights than I cared to admit and constantly oscillated between the foolish hope that everything was going to be fine and accepting the reality that I needed to face.

"I'm a good man," I said to myself out loud.

Why did you do all this? replied the voice in my head. *How could you have been so reckless for so long . . . so out of control? Why can't you just get your shit together?*

And then again out loud: "Who the fuck am I?"

The stench of self-pity smelled about as bad as my car.

You rarely win a debate with yourself, and this one wasn't going to be any different.

I had talked my way out of almost every tight spot I found myself in before, so why not this one? That too was part of the problem. I was a chameleon. I had become so good at lying and manipulating my way out of being seen as the bad guy that I couldn't see I had become the man I was trying to avoid. I didn't want to lie, cheat, hurt other people, yet there I was, still running the mental simulations of how I could maneuver my way through all the damage I caused and remain unscathed.

I was a full-grown man who was terrified of consequences.

I had hit an inflection point, a fork in the road, choose your metaphor. The kind of defining moment that comes along and confronts who you are at your core. I'd been chasing the illusion that someday I would just change. The fantasy that I would miraculously be a "good man" without having to do any of the work to clean up the mess I had made when acting out from the pain I had carried. I bought into the hollowed-out, empty-promise version of life and faith that tells us we can have whatever we want, if we only *believe* hard enough. But all of that had come crashing down. I was finally letting the naive, boyhood notion of living a carefree and consequence-free life die away.

What's the old saying about insanity and doing the same thing over and over? Exactly.

Later that night, as I once again pulled the blanket up over my chest and tried to adjust so the seatbelt buckle didn't dig into my kidney, my gaze wandered out through the back window and caught a glimpse of the sky. It was completely clear, with stars dotting the black void of the moonless night.

I'd spent the past few weeks trying to decide what to do, with zero results. I'd played out thousands of different scenarios, everything from elaborate stories that would get me out of the mess I had made to one-way tickets to Thailand. Tonight, however, as I looked out at the sparkling sky, tears began to stream down my face as I contemplated much darker thoughts.

I was tired. I felt as though the heaviness of my life had its foot planted firmly on my chest and there was no more running. I felt so much shame and anger for the man I had become.

I had no clue what to do next, but I knew I couldn't keep going down the road I was on. It was only going to lead to total self-destruction.

PAIN AS THE PATH

The wounds, scars, and pain we carry as men have a place in our lives. A function that can lead us directly to the core of deep meaning and fulfillment and provide a positive path forward. This is what initiation was *supposed* to teach us as men—how to descend into the depths of our own darkness and return a more complete and contributive participant in society.

However, this is where a man's real problem resides: He has not been taught the skill or alchemy of initiation. He has not learned how to deal with his pain, or the pain of the world, and so he bucks against it.

I realized over the years of grappling with how to heal that not only was I ill-equipped to deal with the hurt I'd been given, but I also seemed to be *woefully* ill-equipped to reconcile with, and put a halt to, the perpetual hurt I passed on to others. Like many men, I was good at inflicting pain—and men who are good at something tend to do that thing a lot.

Not only was I undereducated in the alchemical craft of turning pain into purpose, but almost every man I knew was in relatively the same situation. Most men simply haven't been taught how to deal with their pain and use it to become something better.

And this aspect of the journey is the missing link in male initiation, which has historically played the role of guiding a man through the transitory period between adolescence and adulthood, teaching him the skills of discipline, sovereignty, and the ability to face some of the most challenging aspects of his own life.

In fact, I began to see that not only have most men not been given the tools or resources to deal with the pain and suffering in their lives, but we as men are actively taught the opposite—the idiotic tactic of constant emotional avoidance. Not only this, but our emotional avoidance is seen as a theoretical and rational *strength* in certain circles.

Seeing this brings about a multitude of questions that both illuminate the foundational cracks within current masculine culture and also highlight the work we must embark on if we are to do our individual and collective parts as men in building a thriving society.

There's more: I began to see the direct correlation between a man's ability and willingness to face his own darkness and having a clear purpose, deep fulfillment, and clarity of contribution to the things that matter most to him.

But how can we as men give our pain a purpose in a culture where we are largely devoid of emotional permissions? Where the archetype of man, in order to be classified or quantified as *a* man, must do the impossible task of being brave and courageous without being vulnerable? This is one of the biggest masculine myths—the false idea that you can be courageous without being inherently vulnerable.

When we are rewarded for giving our lives, our hearts, and our emotional bodies up for sacrifice to maintain the illusion of *invulnerable* strength, we prioritize victory over connection. We praise ourselves for performance in the boardroom, bedroom, and bars, but we lack recognition for our performance in reconciliation, repair, and reparation.

There's another way. A way where victory is found within the work, and part of that work is facing our own darkness.

FORGING A NEW WAY

I want to make it clear that this book is a guidebook for *any man* embarking on the journey within. The journey into their own pain, healing, integration, and embodiment—the journey of betterment.

It is meant to acknowledge the pain that we as men carry collectively and individually.

It is meant to showcase the pain we have been given, and have passed on to others, while providing an instructional training manual for transforming this pain into purpose. One that rewards reciprocal relationships, a stronger sense of direction, and a more integrated quality of self-leadership.

The work in this book is work that any man can undertake. It's not meant to be the unequivocal guide and final word. There are many kinds of work that men must face, and many paths he can take. I'm not so arrogant as to believe that the work I've laid out in this book is *the only* path or work a man must do. Rather, this is one man's perspective on the collective work we as men are called to do. It is the conglomeration of more than a decade of learning, listening, apprenticeship, personal work, and experience from the thousands of men I've had the honor of working with.

This book is a map for those wishing to explore masculine darkness and learn how to integrate it into their own being so they are not so controlled by it.

RECONNECTING TO MASCULINITY

This book is unapologetically pro-men and pro-masculinity. It is for men, from men, and about men. It is not in defense of men, or written as an attempt to advocate for men's rights or make excuses for men who act out and cause havoc. It is for the man who wants to heal. The man who is ready to strengthen and embolden himself. The man who is ready to better himself, face his inner demons, and fortify his masculinity.

The truth about masculinity in our modern culture is that it's largely optional. It's no longer necessary. You don't need it in order to survive, fit in, or get by within our postindustrial, globalized complex. You can live your entire life never really needing to know what it's like to live a masculine-oriented life. Hell, some women say they want more effeminate men who are entirely disconnected from their masculine traits (whether or not any of those relationships last or function is a wholly different conversation).

Most men today have never stopped to define their own lives or what masculinity truly means to them. They are bouncing around, out of control, trying to satisfy everyone around them without a clue as to how they can fulfill their inner hunger or stoke the flames of their deepest strength.

Let's make this clear with a few common examples. Do you ever wonder:

— Why you can't fully commit to a relationship, job, or healthy habits?

— Why you're so hard on yourself, and why you can't get your shit together?

— Why the marriage and family you built is out of control and on the brink of falling apart?

— Why you lack purpose, direction, or fulfillment in life?

— Why you don't know what you really want or what makes you happy?

— Why you feel like you have so much anger and need to numb out all the time?

— Why you constantly procrastinate or lack the confidence to do the things you want or need to do?

— Why it feels like you're constantly letting people down?

— "Am I *that guy*?" The guy who can't seem to kick the old habits and is consistently stuck in a cycle of watching too much porn, streaming TV and movies, playing video games, indulging in vices, and avoiding everything else?

— If being you has gotten so bad that you can't peel yourself out of bed in the morning?

— Why you're in a rut of seemingly endless self-sabotage?

— How your sex life is really doing?

Admit it: you've not only asked yourself some or all of these questions, but you've also found yourself swallowed up by them, allowing the existential malaise to bring you down. What if, once and for all, you could finally stand up to your inner critic, stop sabotaging yourself, and be a man you deeply respect? Who do you think you'd become?

What if all the dysfunction, overanalyzing, anxiety, and mental suffering you experience daily could be dealt with in a way that allows you to build your life rather than tear it down?

What if you could finally have the consistent morning routine you crave, understand women on a more intimate level, have the type of sex you desire, the clarity you've been seeking in your career or business, and the financial abundance you know you deserve? What if you had the inner drive to face your fears and banish excuse-making and rationalizations from your daily life? Would you be willing to do the work to have it all?

This is not an attempt at some crappy sales pitch or motivational speech, but rather a mirror for the inner dialogue and desires that have likely plagued your mind. Most men feel a deep sense of disconnection from their own masculinity and masculine core. They are disconnected from their inner compass—their ability to lead, challenge themselves, and expand their capacity as a man, father, and husband.

Most men are looking for freedom. The freedom to lead themselves in a way that is strong, bold, effective, and contributes to the world around them.

This is where the work starts, and it is all centered on facing and integrating what the psychoanalyst Carl Jung called the *shadow*.

Your shadow is the part of your personality where your insecurities, fears, grievances, resentments, and dark impulses not only reside but also tirelessly work to pull you down into the depths of your pain and dysfunction. It is the place where you hide everything you dislike about yourself and least want others to know, and the aspect responsible for sabotaging your best laid plans and intentions.

Men's Work focuses on the growth and expansion that occur when you acknowledge your mistakes, work through past traumas, and remove habitual dysfunction from your life. One of the main aspects of men's work is guiding you to face your shadow and *own all you have neglected, ignored, and avoided*. This is where shadow work comes in. It's the main tool because it helps you understand the hidden drivers behind your sabotage and reckless behaviors, and allows you to form a tactical plan of revealing, understanding, and integrating what had previously been rejected by, hidden from, or unknown to you.

In short, this work is an initiation to help you become the man you're capable of becoming.

The information in this book represents a proven framework to help you break out of the dysfunctional patterns holding you back from the kind of sex, freedom, purpose, and peace you seek—but you'll have to put in the effort. Just thinking about these concepts will not change your behavior, magically solve your problems with women, or give you the mindset and routines you've been wanting to create.

The truth is that you will have to work, and you will face resistance. How you lead yourself through this book and through this work will teach you much about who you really are as a man. And that's the point. It is meant to show you that self-leadership equals freedom, but that freedom isn't always easy to acquire.

At the core of a man's work are two pillars—a magnetic pull toward freedom, and the deep yearning to lead ourselves effectively, with passion, respect, and fulfillment.

Which brings me to the question, *What is self-leadership?* A simple way of defining it: Self-leadership is *your ability to influence and guide yourself toward your highest aims, potential, capabilities, and purpose.* It is your capacity for self-reliance, trust, and direction, regardless of the situation or circumstances. Self-leadership is about being able to regulate your mind, body, and nervous system, while being able to direct yourself toward meaningful aims and outcomes.

The truth is that the more capable and effective you are at leading yourself, the freer you will be and feel. This doesn't mean you need to have all the answers, or always know exactly what to do, but rather that you know you can still thrive in the face of not knowing and deep uncertainty.

Throughout the book I've included "Questions to Answer—Truths to Uncover" and "Integration Exercises" designed to facilitate the paradigm shifts necessary to be a self-led man. These sections will coincide with the content discussed in each chapter, giving you the tools to create real change.

Men's work is less about parsing out what it means to be a man and more centered on exploring the foundational elements of what makes up a man. *It's not simply about being a good man. It's about learning to be good at being a man.*

It involves facing and understanding your own demons, darkness, and the other elements of the shadow: defining and cultivating an authentic presence, freeing trapped emotions, and harnessing their power to allow wisdom and intuition to flourish.

If you're ready to reclaim your life and follow a plan that will change everything, let's begin. Step into the arena.

PART 1

LEADING THROUGH DARKNESS

CHAPTER 1

DISCOVER YOUR SHADOW

"The new man must bear the burden of the shadow consciously, for such a man knows that whatever is wrong in the world is in himself, and if he only learns to deal with his own shadow he has done something real for the world. He has succeeded in shouldering at least an infinitesimal part of the gigantic, unsolved social problems of our day."

CARL JUNG

IT IS USEFUL to know your own darkness. To understand why it exists, what manufactured it, and where it may be slinking into your life, causing chaos and disorder. And this is what the shadow is—the invisible material of chaos, deterioration, and sabotage, coupled with the untapped potential lying dormant within you. Understanding your shadow can do a great many things for you, the least of which is to give you a more robust and complete understanding of who you are and what gives your life meaning. It can also aid in the development of wholeness, fulfillment, humility, and confidence. Simply put, it will help you be a more effective self-led man.

Carl Jung, the eminent Swiss psychiatrist and psychoanalyst, stressed that the individual's goal in life, indeed in becoming more self-led, was to aim for wholeness and not perfection. Jung believed this path to wholeness demanded an individual develop a greater character or more effective approach to life by integrating the elements of the psyche that have been repressed or denied—the elements that make up what Jung called the shadow.

But what is it that we put into our shadows?

It is here that we hide all that is deemed bad or immoral by society, friends, and family. All the traits, values, wants, and desires that we've been ridiculed or punished for, and all the aspects of our personality we have come to dislike. Given that no family or social system is perfect, when adapting to the social world we not only repress the destructive and "unacceptable" elements of our personality, we also end up sacrificing our positive, purpose-oriented characteristics to the shadow's fiery pits. Perhaps your competitiveness and ambition were talked about as a threat, or your assertiveness was punished. Or maybe your creative endeavors were ridiculed, leaving you feeling outcast from a family or peer group. Regardless of the circumstances, most people grow up having to trade some of their authentic strengths and gifts for safety and belonging.

As we repressed elements of our inherent personality, we were morphed into a more timid, tame, or obedient man. A man who was more predictable, "nice," and deemed more likeable. But this repression comes at a cost—it severs a man from his truth, self-respect, vitality, and sense of wholeness. He learns through this act of repression and avoidance not to trust his own instinct, intuition, or sense of direction, and he can begin to live with a deep sense of confusion, often trying to overcompensate for the inner lack of clarity. It is for this very reason that Jung believed unearthing, facing, and integrating the shadow was not only imperative for the individual, but it ultimately leads to his development of self-reliance. And that's what this book will help you do.

Historically, within male culture, darkness and facing darkness has played a significant role in the demarcation between boyhood and manhood. It is also the numinous and enigmatic space which marks a man's maturation. These periods often require us to face some element of truth about ourselves or the world that we had otherwise been ignoring or completely blind to, as is often the case. In this process, some or many parts of our identity will come into question, and the decomposition of who we once were will begin, revealing a new, ideally more unified, robust, and contributive version of our persona.

This is the foundation of what personal, short for personality, development means—to develop your personality. Today "personal development" gets conflated with achieving more material success. However, the origins of personal development are rooted in the maturation and evolution of your persona, which not only requires the cultivation of skills and beliefs that are of higher value to you and those around you, but also the decay and decomposition of the former beliefs, mental constructs, and narratives you held that no longer serve you. Said another way, personal growth isn't *only* about personal becoming; *it is also a process of personal unbecoming.* A process of letting aspects of our personality die away, acting as the fertile soil for the new and more mature version of us to emerge.

So, to know the direction of your becoming is to be forced into contact with the ever-present and often ominous breakdown of what you've known or who you've been. This notion is confronting at best because it forces us to stare into the abyss of the unknown. It causes us to take a 180-degree turn to look deep into the recess of who we have been trying desperately *not* to be.

And this is where the shadow exists. It is the conglomeration of all you have tried not to be, wanted to hide from others, and avoided about yourself. It is the insecurity you hide in your relationships, the neediness you can't control, the lies you tell your family, and the judgment you have toward yourself and others. It is the sabotage that shows up when you most wish to succeed. Or maybe, like me, you grew up in a religious household where anything unsavory about the family that didn't fit into the Bible-ready, priest-acceptable version of what a good Catholic family should look like was swept under the rug, creating a shadow in the household that was almost tangible.

Your shadow consists of all the baggage you've tried to hide from your conscious mind. You're either afraid to express it openly, like a sexual desire or fantasy you won't bring up with your wife because of a past rejection you experienced, or paradoxically you are compelled to reveal it through compulsive behavior, like paying for prostitutes or women online to act out that desire even though you hate yourself for doing so.

Either way, when the shadow is in action, "you" likely feel out of control.

The shadow is also a fitting name because in many ways it consists of all the parts of our psyche and identity that we don't know about, or are too afraid to admit even exist. *It is a literal lack of illumination,* a kind of blind spot, or alter ego.

When you are acting in a self-limiting, self-sabotaging, self-destructive, and self-defeating manner, your shadow is present and likely running the show. It is a kind of splinter personality that aims to prevent you from realizing and actualizing your full potential, largely because your potential has been stashed away in the dark recesses of the shadow, far away from your conscious reach.

The shadow exists for a number of reasons. First, because your ego (or sense of identity) is limited in its bandwidth and generally needs to omit aspects of who you are—especially when those aspects don't fit into how you want to see yourself, or perhaps these parts of you are not accepted by the ruling moral and social standards. For example, one of the ruling social standards our modern culture places upon men is that they should be nice, tame, and agreeable. So, men abandon their divergent or disagreeing nature into the shadow, only to wonder why they are so deeply miserable in the aspects of their lives where they continuously acquiesce to someone else's wants and needs.

Your shadow also exists because during your lifetime, you experience pain and suffering. This pain and suffering—whether it's abuse, abandonment, rejection, loss, or embarrassment—wasn't healed or understood properly, and because of this, the psyche needed to do something with that experience. The shadow, especially within male culture, has become a storehouse of repressed, hidden, and rejected pain. This pain lies in wait and strikes when a man least wants it to—bringing up insecurities and sabotage when he most desires courage and bravery.

Jung believed that in order to navigate the shadow we must first come into contact with it as an intellectual concept. Then, through continuous introspection and reflection, we begin to understand what our own shadow consists of—causing us to awaken to the troubling truth that a portion of our personality is not only at odds with social morality but also at odds with our innate, conscious desires. Said more simply: your shadow is working to sabotage your goals and aims.

The perfect example of this, and one of the most transparent examples of a man and his shadow in modern culture, is personified by the characters of the Narrator and Tyler Durden in *Fight Club* (the film based on the novel by Chuck Palahniuk).

The Narrator, played by Edward Norton, is a repressed, mundane, and melancholy insomniac who is the literal definition of a domesticated man. So hopelessly lacking in any kind of solidified identity and actual substance, the main character, the person who is at the very center of the entire story, is so lost and unaware of who he is that his name is never revealed—a clear and direct signal of his missing identity. He has spent a lifetime abiding the whims of culture, bosses, and girlfriends and has never really developed anything within himself, outside of the almost palpable self-loathing.

Nothing in his life looks the way he wants it to, but he also seems largely incapable of doing anything about it. The Narrator's personality can be summed up in one sentence when he says, while sitting on the toilet attempting to find meaning in his life by ordering furniture from an Ikea catalog, "I flip through catalogs and wonder, what kind of dining set defines me as a person?" And while sitting on the toilet ordering furniture from a catalog might not be relatable, today's man numbs out by doomscrolling through social media or mindlessly swiping through some dating app attempting to find validation of who he is based on who he can get into his bed.

Then enters Tyler Durden's character (played by Brad Pitt). Tyler is abrasively confident, bold, unapologetic, and ruthless in his self-assuredness. He has no doubt about who he is and what he wants, and he is quite literally the antithesis of the Narrator's character. Tyler is the physical and psychological manifestation of everything the Narrator has avoided and wants to be—no fucks, no worries, anti-establishment, and pro-self-interest.

Over the course of the film, you watch as the Narrator's identity erodes and dies off, slowly being replaced by the beliefs, behaviors, and actions of Tyler Durden. The Narrator, who has never really had a sure sense of who he is at his core, adopts more and more of Durden's persona and carries out his marching orders, absolving himself from the life he had been living. As Durden's plans and desires escalate to an almost maniacal level, the Narrator finds his interests and ability to agree with Durden beginning to fade.

Finally, in a raw and panicked moment, the Narrator's reality cracks when he finds out there may be no Tyler Durden. Or, more accurately, there may be no Tyler Durden other than the Narrator himself. After he calls Marla, the woman Tyler had been sleeping with, she confirms that he, the Narrator, is in fact Tyler Durden. Or at least had been parading around as him. Suddenly Tyler appears in the room with the Narrator and conflict ensues as the Narrator's reality collapses around him.

Now, to be clear, the Narrator in the film had a psychotic break, probably due to insomnia. But on a symbolic level, Tyler Durden is the psychological and physical manifestation of the Narrator's shadow, personified and externalized for the Narrator and viewer to see what a real, legitimized alter ego can look like. Tyler is everything the Narrator has repressed, hidden, and rejected about himself. Tyler represents the masculine qualities the Narrator has abandoned—freedom, boldness, assertiveness, clarity, and direction. Tyler was a conglomeration of all the elements, behaviors, and desires the Narrator had repressed, a kind of projection he wished he could be.

While your shadow is likely not externalized like that of the Narrator, it is still, in the words of Jung, the archetype or aspect that shows up as the "unconscious snag, thwarting your most well-meant intentions."

Facing your shadow means facing your cowardice, envy, laziness, ignorance, dishonesty, insecurities, greed, lust, vanity, and other self-indulgent tendencies, which will have to be navigated directly. However, it is on this quest where we as men begin to discover our true sense of sovereignty, strength, meaning, confidence, purpose, and direction. This is the paradoxical nature of life and the psyche: to know life in all of its richness, we must also be conscious of death and its ever-present wisdom. So the question is: Are you really ready to know yourself? Are you ready to face and confront the truth about who you've been and want to become? If so, read on.

WHAT'S NEEDED FOR MEN'S WORK

To do this work, you will need a few tools for the journey.

— Willingness to be honest and transparent, even when it's uncomfortable (this is a big one)

— Deep exploration of one's personal history to understand the origins and formation of behavioral patterns and belief systems—not just from an intellectual space but also through an experiential lens

— An agreement to get out of your head and into your body, into the emotional and experiential data of your life

— A commitment to self-reflection and a willingness to discover and disclose what has been hidden

— Dedication to absolute ownership; as in, being able to admit when you've deviated, become reactive, or are avoiding/rejecting what's true or necessary

Now, to understand the shadow, it's important to know what's waiting for you inside it. Your shadow might include things like:

Anger / Assertiveness. For some men, their anger is hidden in the shadow, and for others it is the weapon of the shadow.

Limiting beliefs. These are self-defeating and destructive narratives about who we are.

Fear. This can be the anxiety-fueled voice constantly worrying and warning us of dangers that don't even exist.

Shame. When we feel embarrassed, humiliated, rejected, or as though we have let others down. Shame is a suppressant like alcohol and can numb us out to our other emotions, wants, and needs.

Sexual desires. We may feel shame for our wants and desires, so we hide them away. Often they emerge one way or another, and usually in unhealthy ways.

Grief. This is felt especially when we minimize the impact of a loss or failure. Many men have stored the grief of their past failures, heartbreaks, neglects, and abandonments in their shadow.

Purpose. This involves gaining a sense of the direction your life is meant to take. What you are meant to contribute, build, and create can all be revealed from the shadow.

Potential. This is a *big* one. Many men will store the true depths of their potential away in their shadow. They express not knowing what they are capable of, not believing they'll ever "get there," and feeling a chasm between who they are now and who they think they should be or need to become.

Joy. For some, their willingness to express or experience joy is hidden away, especially when they have a conscious narrative of not deserving joy, or a worry that they will be the cause of joy's destruction.

Boundaries. Some will avoid setting boundaries so their intentions and desires are hidden, while others will set fierce boundaries, often with the same effect.

QUESTIONS TO ANSWER ▸ TRUTHS TO UNCOVER

Continue each statement below, finding your own answers. Let your answers be as long as feels natural and necessary.

What I don't like others to know about my past is . . .

What I least want people to know about me is . . .

What I often hide about myself to gain social acceptance is . . .

What I hide about my current or past relationship is . . .

When someone disagrees with me, I feel . . .

The emotion I tend to hide from others is . . .

The emotion I least like to express to my partner is . . .

My father said being a man is . . .

My mother said being a man is . . .

What I've been avoiding in my life/relationship is . . .

I don't like to talk about my . . .

My anger is . . .

I lose control of my anger when . . .

I'm quick to judge others for . . .

My potential is . . .

When I'm stressed I deal with it by . . .

Answering these questions feels . . .

INTEGRATION EXERCISE

Part of a man's work is facing the hard things he wants to avoid.

Start by making a list of everything you've been avoiding lately. Conversations, people, experiences, taxes, habits, routines, apologies, all of it. Then pick one thing that you've been avoiding from the list and make a declaration to act on it this week.

INTEGRATION EXERCISE

Write down one to three people or groups that may be able to provide accountability and support in doing this work. One of the main goals of the shadow is to stay hidden, so your work is about revealing, reconciling, and reclaiming what you have stored there. This means going through this work with another man, men's group, counsellor, coach, twelve-step group, or therapist. If you don't have any support, join the ManTalks Alliance—an online group with hundreds of men from around the world doing this work (mantalks.com/the-alliance/).

Now commit to reaching out to them within the next seventy-two hours and enlisting their support. Be clear with your ask and expectations.

REVEALING THE UNSEEN MAN WITHIN

For years I saw a client, David, who struggled to take hold of the life he wanted for himself.

He didn't feel happy with his job even though he worked for one of the most prominent companies in the world, felt at the whim of the women he dated, and continued to express his dissatisfaction with 90 percent of his life. He had big dreams and aspirations for himself but felt as though his life was largely being lived based on other people's wants and needs. He had trouble saying no to the women he dated, stayed in relationships longer than he wanted, and even though he had the financial capacity to leave his nine-to-five and start his own business, he wasn't able to bridge the gap between who he was and who he wanted to be.

On the outside he was an incredibly smart, talented, and driven man who had come from extreme poverty and worked his way up the corporate ladder to financial independence, and he was well-liked by most. He grew up in a remote part of northern Canada far away from any real form of modern civilization. He never knew his birth father as his mother had a one-night stand turned first-born child, and he found himself caught in a home with a stepfather who made it blatantly obvious that David was not a welcome part of the family.

When we started working together, David kept talking about what he wished he could do. What he wanted to do. How he never really felt like he was able to show the real version of himself to the people around him.

As a child David had been largely left to fend for himself against the constant, and often unannounced, verbal attacks from his stepfather. He was always on the lookout from a young age and quickly learned his mere presence could cause his stepfather to erupt into a fit of yelling, name calling, and verbal threats.

When asked what it was like to be around that kind of parent, he said, "It was like being an American covert op in Russia during the Cold War. I was paranoid, lived on a constant diet of fear soup, and spent most of my waking hours trying to figure out what I needed to do or be in order to avoid his wrath."

David had learned that it wasn't okay to be himself and that in order to fit in (or in his case, survive) he needed to suppress his own wants, needs, and truth. Because of this he would often fantasize about *massive* action and *monumental* change. We dubbed this the "lottery mindset," something many men will recognize in themselves. He had fallen into the trap of having to suppress himself as a means of survival when he was a boy and believed that the only way out of his current predicament was to do something drastic like quit his job, buy a one-way ticket to Thailand, and abandon everything he had built.

While working with David I began to learn that what he feared most was revealing who he truly was. Partially because he didn't know what it was like to live a life based on his own terms, but also because he had been punished for being who he was as a child. This left David largely hating who he was as he had adopted an incredibly negative and self-demeaning mindset because of the environment he grew up in. At first David would bring his problems and decisions into our sessions and would use his wit and intelligence to try and get me to make decisions for him. I learned that even if it took weeks of discussing the same issue with him as he ran through the multitude of potential pitfalls and possible failed outcomes, the best thing I could do for him was to help him repair his ability to know that it was safe for him to act on what he thought was best for himself and his life. He had never learned to trust himself or his decisions, and it was crippling his confidence.

Slowly over the course of months, we worked on having him make small, incremental decisions that were solely based on his internal sense of what he wanted for himself. Eventually David built a foundation of trust within himself and decided to leave his job, start his own business, and travel for months while working from wherever he wanted.

Now, not all men have had David's circumstances, but many have their own stories of learning to shut up, keep quiet, and stuff it down.

John is a perfect example. He loved his father and idolized him. When John was a child, John's father was strict, disciplined, and rarely showed any flaws. His father was a blue-collar worker in a local automotive factory and was intensely disciplined in his routines and habits, often reminding John that discipline was crucial for survival. Watching his father enact his ceremonial morning shave, his workout routine, and the smell of his coffee with oatmeal every day for the first eighteen years of his life were childhood memories John still looked back on as deeply meaningful.

"When I lost my dad, I felt like I lost my best friend," John said to me in one of our early sessions. "He really was an incredible man. I had the deepest respect for him and have worked tirelessly to be half the man he was, which is why losing him has been so fucking hard. It's like I've lost my anchor in some ways."

John had come to see me not only because he had lost his father, but because he was miserable since his father's death and had largely been unable to grieve.

"I'm angry. Like rage-filled. I don't want to talk to my wife, everything she does and says annoys me, and every time my son cries it makes me want to punch a hole through the wall," he admitted in our first conversation.

John was stuck. He was unable to grieve his father's passing and, in my terms, was emotionally constipated.

He had lost an icon, yet he said he wasn't sad. He was confused about how he was supposed to be handling his father's death. On one hand he held the belief that his father's death shouldn't affect him, and on the other he held the truth that he felt on the brink of complete devastation.

"My old man would have a lot to say if he saw me sitting here in your office," John quipped.

"Why's that?" I inquired.

"Because he thought therapy was pointless and a waste of time. My dad used to say it was a place for women to complain about their husbands, and that if a man couldn't sort out his problems on his own, he wasn't a real man. Women talk, men act, he used to say."

"Good thing I'm not a therapist," I replied, eliciting a chuckle and gaining a better understanding of why he had sought me out.

During one of our sessions, I was walking John through an exercise to help him connect to the grief of losing his father. At one point he described feeling as though there was a battle between the man he needed to be for his father and the man he was.

"I can feel this weight in my chest, like an anvil of sadness pinning me down, but I can't seem to get it out or get it off of me," John said.

"Imagine your father is in the room with us," I said. "What would he say about that anvil?"

John was silent for a few moments. His breathing seemed to halt almost entirely as tension built in the muscles around his shoulders, chest, and neck.

Finally, he replied, "He'd probably say it's the cost of being a man. That I need to learn to be strong enough to carry it."

"And what about that weight?" I replied. "What does the weight in your chest want to say back to him?"

Again silence. John's face began to contort slightly. His eyebrows crinkled and quivered, cheeks tightened, and the muscles in his neck strained as if he was working with his entire being to swallow that weight back down into the depths of his being.

"It would say that I don't want to carry it the same way he did."

"Can you tell him that directly?" I asked.

Now tears were streaming down John's face. He sat in perfect stillness. Fists clenched, breath shallow, and face still contorted, attempting to block the grief rushing forth.

"I don't want to carry this shit like you did, Dad. I don't want to stuff it down and pretend like I'm not fucking sad you're gone. I'm tired of having to hide it. I saw what it did to you," John proclaimed.

We spent the next few sessions talking about how much John missed his father and how he had been searching for permission to grieve. John also disclosed that he thought he needed to suppress many different aspects of who he was just to gain his father's approval. He had worked tirelessly to gain the respect of a man he deeply admired, but it came at the cost of his own emotional well-being. The unseen man within John craved a more robust relationship with his own son but didn't know how to access it.

Now, this work was not about tarnishing his father or making him the villain. John's father was still an incredible man, role model, and parent. It was simply an awakening to the reality that John's dad, while exceptional in many ways, still had his flaws in John's eyes. And that part of John's reconciliation with the death of his father was embedded in his ability to own this truth, allowing him to connect to the unseen, hidden man within he'd locked away in order to gain his father's approval and respect.

REPRESSION AND SUPPRESSION: HOW THE MAN WITHIN STAYS HIDDEN

Within all men is a hidden man.

An unseen man.

A man who, at some point in his life, bought into the narrative that *suppression equals strength and survival.*

For many men, suppression has become a way of life.

It's become the norm for the man who feels like an imposter at work or doesn't feel like he deserves the relationship he's in, or for the man who constantly sabotages his own personal betterment at every turn.

Just like David and John had to reclaim the aspects of their true nature that had been abandoned or sacrificed in the name of acceptance, you too will be faced with the task of reclamation. As you read their stories you likely felt the pull within from atomized aspects of your own identity. Creative desires, unfulfilled dreams, hidden griefs, and unmet emotions you've stuffed deep in the pockets of your psyche in an attempt to fit in or survive.

For a moment, let yourself make contact with and think about the man you hide from the people around you. The man you don't want others to know about, see, or discover. Who is he? What does he want? When does he show up, and why is he there? Is he someone you want to spend time with, or someone you wish you could kill off? And what would others say if they met him?

Often, the unseen man within is a culmination of all the aspects of himself he believes need to be hidden to belong in male culture or be seen as desirable to women.

He is some combination of what a man has had to hide, reject, and avoid—the things he hates about himself and wishes didn't exist. The unseen man is a prisoner within you and often holds the keys to your sense of liberation.

This unseen man is built through the tedious and repetitive pressure of *repression* and *suppression.*

Repression, as I'm using it, is when some external force (a parent, colleague, group, bullies, or social narrative) puts you into a state of submission, causing you to reject, hide, or diminish something true (emotions, experience, desires, etc.). Maybe you were bullied into compliance and forced to hide your anger, or told you'd be rejected from the family if you pursued a certain career or passion, causing you to dim the bright light of your creativity.

Suppression, as I'm using it, is a mechanism where you as an individual choose to hide, diminish, or reject something as a means of self-preservation, social acceptance, or gaining perceived status. This suppression is meant to help protect you, allow you to fit in, or give the illusion of strength and competence.

Both suppression and repression are the enemies of a self-led man. They weaken a man's resolve, causing him to live in fear of himself. They encourage and entice a man to withhold his truth and bury his fears out of sight, blinding him to the path he is meant to walk. The psychological territory of suppression is a wasteland of shame, resentment, and insecurity. It is the psychospiritual force that acts as an ever-tightening rear naked choke hold on a man's identity, slowly crushing the windpipe of his freedom and confidence, cutting off the blood flow to his ability to trust his own choices.

Where there is suppression, there is a wounded and weakened man on his knees acting from fear, pain, and half-strength.

Now, with all of this in mind, I want to make one thing clear. Suppression and repression are separate from the things we withhold because they are inappropriate, could be damaging, or are socially unacceptable. Sometimes we need to withhold the comment about how attractive we find our boss or coworker, and we need to refrain from making wildly inappropriate comments in certain social situations. This is the distinction between suppressing or repressing and keeping ourselves in check.

Revealing the repressed and suppressed parts of you is essential. It will force you to come face to face with the aspects of yourself that have been abandoned and discarded. It will make you bear witness to and commune with the parts you normally hide from the people around you.

Revealing what is suppressed and hidden in you is essential to your sense of belonging. Indeed, it is vital for your very capacity to love and be loved, to lead yourself and lead others, and is rooted in the caliber and quality of our transparency. Said another way, *we only trust that we belong to the degree we are willing to risk being known.* Transparency, courageous honesty, and revealing the core of our inner truth is essential for combating the ever-present psychological compression caused by the gravitational weight of suppression.

Come back into contact with your unseen man. What have you been suppressing or hiding recently in your life that you would like to take ownership of? If that unseen man had a voice and could speak, what would he say or ask for? For the next week, challenge yourself to act on revealing this part. That might mean owning something you've been avoiding, apologizing for a certain behavior, having a hard conversation you've been neglecting to have, or simply telling the truth about what you've wanted.

If you'd like to learn more about your unseen man, dig into the questions below. Don't worry so much about having the perfect answer; simply allow yourself to notice what comes into your mind as you read the question.

QUESTIONS TO ANSWER ▸ TRUTHS TO UNCOVER

The boy/man I was told (directly or indirectly) I needed to be was . . .

The boy/man I was told (directly or indirectly) *not* to be was . . .

What I didn't want my parents to know about me was . . .

I felt like I had no choice growing up when . . .

As a kid I rebelled against . . .

I was punished for . . .

What I thought I had to hide from my parents was . . .

What I didn't want my friends to know about me growing up was . . .

Today what I hide from people is . . .

I don't want my friends, family, or partner to know about . . .

The unseen man within me is . . .

He's afraid of . . .

He wants . . .

CHAPTER 2

THE MYTH OF MALE SEPARATION

"Men build too many walls and not enough bridges."

JOSEPH FORT NEWTON

A MAN'S STRENGTH resides in his capacity to attach to what matters most. Said another way, all aspects of life require a man to learn how to connect or be in relationship with them—purpose, love, discipline, freedom, passion, and sex all demand that a man learns the valuable skill of connection, or he will inevitably feel unable to powerfully affect and influence the aspects of life he deeply craves. As a general rule, what a man connects to, he cares about and cares for.

Even within the realm of elite soldiers like Navy Seals, connecting with and focusing on others is used as a means of stress reduction. Seals go through rigorous training to learn tools like situational awareness—not only how to read the environment they're in, but also how to read and connect to the people around them. The most effective teams are composed of men who have trained themselves to stay in contact with one another—to read the body language, movement, eye contact, and even breathing patterns of their fellow Seal. The best teams move as one because they are deeply connected. They move, feel, operate, and execute their mission not as individual soldiers, but as a collective, all deeply in tune with one another.

However, this is not the case for countless men who have adopted the lone wolf, figure-it-out-yourself mentality. A man's refusal to see himself as an ecological part of a system is also at the core of a man's suffering and work. Whether he believes he is outside of the system entirely, ruling it from above as a dictator or authoritarian would, or beneath it, feeling like a slave to its whims, he will feel powerless to influence or affect the very thing he is a part of. This separation can dramatically impact the way a man engages with his relationships, problems, finances, health, family, and purpose.

The myth of male separation says that *you are a stronger man for separating from anything that might weaken you or cause others to perceive you as weak*. The myth of male separation teaches you to disconnect, desecrate, and dominate anything that may be a threat to your masculinity—be it creativity, sadness, grief, trauma, mother nature, women, or other men.

Because of this myth, countless boys and men will embark on a journey, attempting to detach themselves from anything that could possibly be perceived as weak, defective, or lead to defeat. This cuts a man off from the integral experiences he requires in order to develop a deep trust in his ability to face the fullness of life, which is a part of the masculine drive.

Now, this is not advocating for a female-centric view of men or masculinity. In fact, quite the contrary, as the myth of male separation is frequently adopted and enlisted by certain feminine narratives. Women use this myth against men, flipping it on its head, using it to separate men from valuable masculine traits women deem to be threatening or unnecessary. You've likely heard this in the all-too-common narratives advocating for men to be more vulnerable and agreeable, preaching the value of being emotional with and around women while degrading the importance of traits like being assertive and disagreeable when necessary.

Countless modern men have become highly domesticated and dislodged from their assertiveness and directness when they attempt to conform to the ever-changing and elusive definition of what women think a man should be. When a man tries to build his masculine essence or foundation of maleness on the notion of what women think a man should be, he will flounder. He will hear opposing stories about how men should be "nice guys" and should be largely agreeable to women and a woman's wants in a relationship—while also hearing how women want strong, confident, independent, and assertive men. This contradiction leads men down the path of least resistance as it seems easier to separate from the masculine traits that may lead to conflict or confrontation and acquiesce to the narrative of being a "good guy."

This separation, regardless of where it has come from, is not only at the root of a man's suffering, it is also responsible for the mass confusion men are experiencing in our culture today—feeling torn between the extremes of what a man should be, or more aptly put, what a man should distance himself from.

Much like I had to learn not to separate from what mattered to me, what I feared, and the aspects of myself that I didn't know how to deal with, you too will have to learn how to make contact with the various parts of yourself that may seem unsavory, intolerable, or hard to handle. But don't worry, you won't be alone in the journey. So long as you break the one rule of men.

BREAKING THE ONE RULE OF MEN

A few weeks after my stay in the Walmart parking lot, I found myself sitting across from one of my closest friends. This was a man I had gone through school with and come to appreciate deeply for his impeccable intelligence, wit, and uncanny ability to retain and recall information in a way I didn't think was possible in any human being. He and I had travelled together, spent countless occasions philosophizing about life over the best bottle of scotch we could afford (which wasn't much), and enjoyed what I thought was a deep understanding of who the other man truly was.

It had been a while since we had seen one another, but after some initial barbing and terrible jokes, we began catching up over the events of the last several months.

"So," he said, "how have you been?"

It was a loaded question because the truth was, I had been terrible. My entire life had recently fallen apart, and few people knew about the lies, infidelities, and shame I had been steeped in.

"Honestly," I replied, "not great."

"The truth is," I continued, "I've been a real piece of shit and have a lot to atone for. I've been lying to you and everyone around me."

We sat for what felt like hours as I described what had been going on in the background of my life for the past few years. It was an uncomfortable kind of admission as some of my actions involved people he knew, mutual friends and colleagues we had worked with. I had been having an affair with a colleague that had destroyed my relationship, lied to him about what was happening in my life, and was finally coming clean about my actions. He listened patiently, occasionally sympathizing with what I had gone through.

We sat in silence after I had come to what felt like a reasonable place to stop. It was tense, and I was concerned he was going to tell me to fuck off and get out of his life. Instead, he said something I wasn't expecting.

"Thank you for telling me that. I knew something was going on, but we never seemed to be able to talk about it. In all honesty, I haven't told you the truth about what I've been dealing with either."

My body tensed as I wondered what he could be talking about. I watched as he shifted in his seat, clearly uncomfortable about what he was about to say. My mind immediately went to betrayal, wondering if he had been sleeping with my ex or had screwed me over in some way.

"I honestly don't know how to even say this, but after hearing about what you've been dealing with, I don't feel like I have anything to hide." He paused again, anxiously picking at his nails, trying to find the words.

"I guess there's no easy way to say it, but over the last few months I've been dealing with pretty severe depression. I didn't think much of it at first, but it got worse and worse. I didn't say anything to you, or anyone for that matter, because I didn't want the empty words or pity from people and thought I could deal with it by myself. But it got bad. Like real bad. I started thinking about not being here anymore and wanted to find a way out. Needless to say, about a month ago I tried to end it. End me. I tried to hang myself," he said about as quickly as one could when disclosing this kind of information.

"You tried to kill yourself?" I spit out.

"Yeah, I guess I did. Clearly didn't work though." He forced out an awkward chuckle, trying to break the tension.

We sat for the next few hours discussing what had led us down our individual paths to rock bottom. I couldn't help but feel an unusual cocktail of deep rage mixed with clear compassion and a satisfying finish of relief. The transparency and realness of our conversation was invigorating and revitalizing.

I don't remember all the details of what was said, but I clearly remember sitting there thinking about how close I had thought he and I were. I truly believed I had known everything about this man—his favorite scotch, music, the kind of women he liked to date. Yet clearly we'd been living in a pseudo-friendship where the most important aspects of what we were actually dealing with internally as men were buried deep within each of us, far away from one another.

As the years would pass and I put on events around the world, engaging men in more blunt and transparent dialogue, I came to find that this was all too common. Lifelong friends who didn't know about the affair, deep depression, anxiety, failing business, sexless marriage, or repeated health scares. *Men had depthless friendships.* Some had women they talked to and opened up to, but most lacked in real, depth-oriented male friendships, and it was literally killing them.

This is what I would come to refer to as "the One Rule of Men." The rule is simple: *Don't talk about what it's like to be a man who is struggling.* Don't engage in conversation about the failing marriage, the grief of having a parent die, or the shame of having a business on the brink of collapse. Suck it up. Stuff it down. Deal with it like a man—alone. Sure, you can bitch and complain about the details—offloading your anger about a boss or work situation, maybe even complaining about your wife or girlfriend—but don't share the gravity of what it's like to actually be in that situation.

This is the one rule in life you must absolutely break. In fact, breaking this rule is imperative to your health, fulfillment, and well-being as a man. Find men who are dedicated to self-betterment, men who are willing to not only have the brutally honest conversations but are also willing to take action to rectify what's happening. Find men who are willing to engage in this kind of conversation and to hold you accountable to the change you say you want to create. Do not settle for men who will simply listen to your complaints week after week—surround yourself with men who will call you forward into action (a concept we will talk about later in the book).

Look at the caliber of men surrounding you in daily life. Do you have a deep sense of reverence toward them? If they gave you advice or insight, would you respect it enough to take action? Have you helped those men in return? There are many places where you can find these kinds of conversations. Countless spaces where you can speak with brutal honesty and be met with it in return. It is this kind of candid conversation that most modern men are malnourished in and craving, yet that they are afraid to engage in.

This week, challenge yourself to break the rule. Have a conversation with a close friend about where you've been struggling, share a problem you've been dealing with, or shed light on what you've been trying to deal with alone. Maybe it's your porn habit, the amount of weed you've been smoking, or how miserable things have been in your marriage.

Whatever it is you reveal, I challenge you to break the one rule of men—or suffer from the law of isolation.

QUESTIONS TO ANSWER ▸ TRUTHS TO UNCOVER

The aspects or parts of my life I least like to talk about are . . .

The emotion(s) that I think make(s) me weak is . . .

How I avoid this emotion is . . .

The impact this avoidance has on my life is . . .

I feel disconnected from my partner/spouse when . . .

I felt disconnected from my parents/family as a kid when . . .

The problems or challenges I least want to talk about are . . .

The problems or challenges I'm always talking about are . . .

Answering these questions has revealed . . .

THE LAW OF ISOLATION

Isolation makes a man impotent. Not sexually impotent necessarily, but impotent in the sense that it castrates his ability to connect to the ecosystems, social structures, and communities he would otherwise be able to contribute to. This in turn will cripple a man in his ability to lead in most areas of his life, because this is what leadership is—a process of influencing one or many toward a common goal or task. So, when a man isolates himself from his wife, family, workplace, or community, he disconnects himself from influencing the people, relationships, and environments that matter most to him. It also cuts him off from being influenced, loved, and valued in the way he craves.

As Henry Cloud said, "There is a difference between solitude and isolation. One is connected and one isn't. Solitude replenishes, isolation diminishes."

Isolation creates hopeless and controlling men. It breeds emotionally fragile men who seek to control women, children, employees, friends, and family members as a means of trying to maintain the facade of closeness, ultimately reinforcing their inability to deeply connect and be in relationships.

Isolation builds spiritually bankrupt men who are unable to connect to some form of a "higher power" or benefit from the soul-expanding experience of being in relationship to awe and wonder, which humble a man's ego and work to tether him to the mysteries of the universe. Without this, a man can get deeply lost in the cemented rigidity of his own ego, which itches constantly like an addict for its fix of certainty.

This impotence is caused by what I refer to as "the Law of Isolation." This law states that the inevitable impact of isolation is the amplification of pre-existing conditions, behaviors, thought patterns, emotions, and fears. In its simplest form, this law can be summarized as *isolation equals amplification.*

When you isolate, you are left with nothing but your thoughts, emotions, beliefs, and coping mechanisms—letting them spin out into larger, more robust, and more concrete illusions. Anxiety, depression, imposter syndrome, and the coping mechanisms used to deal with these experiences are all amplified when you isolate from others or attempt to mask your own truth and desires.

Bad eating habits, excessive porn watching, anxieties, and relational dysfunction all increase when a man isolates himself.

However, this isolation was built to do one of two things: *to protect or to punish.*

Some men learned early on that isolation was the safest, most effective way to protect themselves or the ones they loved from harm. For others, isolation was the punishment they received, or thought they should receive, for their failure or wrongdoing.

Craig's father would ignore him for days whenever they would get into a disagreement. Even when Craig would try to apologize or reconnect after the disagreement, his father would walk away and watch TV for hours alone in the den, making sure no one in the family disturbed him, a behavior Craig would painfully replicate in his marriage for years. Craig isolated to punish.

When he was a child, Eric's single mother would lock him in his room for hours at a time with no toys, books, or anything to do when he had done something wrong, telling him it was "for his own protection." As an adult, Eric became somewhat reclusive and found himself checking out from his friend group for weeks at a time, sitting at home smoking weed or binging TV shows after a hard breakup or rough week at work. Eric isolated to punish himself.

When Tim's anger came out as a child, his mother would tell him he had no reason to be angry and that *good boys and strong men don't get angry*. So Tim learned to isolate his anger from the world and his relationships in order to gain approval. He found himself in a marriage with a woman who had a lot of anger, and rather than learn how to set boundaries with her and her anger (which would require him to connect to his own anger), he would shut down and tune out—sometimes making passive aggressive comments, internally judging his wife, wishing she could "just get her shit together." Tim isolated to protect himself and punish his wife.

Notice how all of these men were taught isolation as a means of protection or punishment? They learned from a young age that it was easier to disconnect than it was to remain connected and largely grew up in environments where the safest way to deal with problems was to either shut down, not bring it up, or remove themselves entirely.

Not to be confused with solitude, which can be invigorating and restorative, isolation is destructive in a number of ways. Arguably its most lethal attribute is its ability to amplify what is already present physically, mentally, emotionally, and spiritually. Its primary outcome is the exaggeration of what we have least wanted to face: anxiety, depression, fear, limiting beliefs, worry, doubt, distraction, and unhealthy coping mechanisms ranging from binge eating to excessive porn consumption are all amplified when we isolate.

This isolation serves erroneous beliefs like the following:

— "I can keep others safe by hiding my own truth, emotions, or wants."

— "I am better off alone," or, "It's easier for me to be alone."

— "When I've done something wrong, I deserve to be alone."

— "It is safer for me to be disconnected than connected."

— "I can get my needs met by hiding my perceived flaws."

— "Hiding (isolating) my flaws/needs/emotions will get me the love and connection I want."

— "I can fix my problems (protect myself) or the problems of others (protect others) by removing myself from the experience or hiding how I truly feel about the experience."

Now, think about how often you use isolation as a tactic to deal with your challenges, failures, or worries. When you and your wife or girlfriend haven't had sex in weeks and it feels like you're beginning to question the relationship altogether, what's your first response? Do you lean into the discomfort of having a tough conversation? Do you stay open physically, emotionally, and mentally so you maintain the connection? Or do you go deeper into the pit of despair by spending hours doomscrolling through social media, fire up your favorite Pornhub video, or give her the silent treatment?

The reality is that when we isolate, our propensity toward existing coping mechanisms is heightened and we are more susceptible to negative thought patterns, beliefs, and internal narratives. Simply put, without healthy social connection or our normal community interaction, we are left with nothing but ourselves (and the rabbit hole of the Internet) to deal with.

You will reclaim your power and potency when you choose to turn toward the things you isolate yourself from. Bringing forward and expressing what we've been taught to withhold is not an easy task by any means. Any man who has tried to do this will have surely come into contact with a part of his shadow and its conniving ways. You may have convinced yourself that it's easier to hide what you need or desire, and you could be right about this. In many cases it is indeed easier to close ourselves off from the harsh realities of the world. Life can become more palatable in some respects when we withhold the uncomfortable truths about who we are and what we want and confine ourselves to a life of withdrawal and retreat.

Claim fully and to the best of your capacity in each moment what you most want to hide from the world. Stay close to the parts of your inner world that least want your friends or wife to know about them. If you don't cut through the urge to detach, you place the responsibility on others to save you and solicit what you want. Rather than making people guess where you stand or what direction you wish to move in, let it be known. Do not let yourself be bamboozled by the notion that your woman, friends, or community are better off without your full force and presence.

Do not retreat. Plant your feet firmly in the rich soil of knowing your worth and value as a man. Stand up for yourself and to yourself by marching yourself knowingly and actively in the opposite direction of isolation. Where you would normally close off and become emotionally cold, stay open to the heat of the moment or argument. Replenish your reserves and resiliency in the act of bringing the fullness of who you are out into the world, letting acts of expression, honesty, and honoring yourself shape you and your impact on the world.

QUESTIONS TO ANSWER ▸ TRUTHS TO UNCOVER

First, complete the following statements.

I tend to isolate when . . .

I cut others off when I feel . . .

In those moments I'm trying to protect myself/them from . . .

This feels familiar to . . .

What I usually need in those moments is . . .

What I wish other people knew in those moments was . . .

Next, in a journal, write about what you had to ignore, sacrifice, or neglect in order to fit into your family. What needs or wants did you have to ignore in order to get love and acceptance from your parents, and how did you have to perform in order to get love and approval?

INTEGRATION EXERCISE

This is a practice in maintaining connection. In order to move away from isolation and separation, we need to practice staying in contact—emotionally, physically, psychologically—with the people around us. Next time you are around your partner or someone you feel close to, connect to your breath and bring your consciousness lower into your body. Allow your feet to feel rooted and solid in the ground, maybe even feeling like the breath is coming up through your feet and legs. Maintain a deep connection to the ground and let your awareness move down into your abdomen, and notice the sensations you experience in the body. Stay connected to your breath and relax the muscles in your chest, shoulders, and face. Now that your awareness is deep in the body, let it expand out beyond you, making contact with the other person, and notice the connection you feel to them. What do you sense from them? Are they tense? Is there a certain emotion they are expressing? What about their body language? Is their breath shallow and quick, or deep and relaxed? Stay in contact with them without needing to do anything about where they are at. No need to fix, solve, or alter anything. Simply stay with the breath, slowing it down, consciousness low in the body, staying connected to what arises in the moment of connection.

CHAPTER 3

SHADOW OF THE FATHER

"What was silent in the father speaks in the son;
and often I found in the son the unveiled secret of the father."

FRIEDRICH NIETZSCHE

THE SHADOW OF your father is neither good nor bad, only inescapable. Whether it is the complete absence of your father, his abusive behavior, lackadaisical approach to life, or the monumental greatness he stood for in your eyes as his son, part of a man's work will inevitably lead him on a collision course with the shadow his father cast.

No man will be able to claim the throne of his own inner kingdom without knowing and stepping outside of his father's. This is the irony of the father archetype—that in order to gain individual maturity, a man must separate from his father, carving out his own path and sovereignty in the world, only to reconnect later as his own individual man. This becomes challenging when a man has blinded himself to the real impact and role his father has played.

When a boy is young he looks up to his father, witnessing the larger-than-life figure who is meant to symbolize and be the primary archetype of masculinity, order, direction, and guidance. It gives the boy a sense of what lies beyond his current state as a child and paints an image of who or what he could become as he enters into manhood. In biblical texts and mythological literature the father is the bringer of order. He is tasked with transmuting chaos into something more clear, concise, and structured. This brings peace, harmony, and balance to the family, village, and world.

However, many men wish to write off their fathers, hoping to diminish their impact, not knowing that to put down, resent, or pedestal the father handicaps their own development as a son.

The adolescent angst of many men presumes to know how their fathers should have reared them. They judge their fathers heavily for how they parented—projecting their childhood wants and needs onto their fathers well into adulthood, sometimes carrying resentment even after their fathers have passed. "Why didn't he spend more time with me?" or "Why didn't he teach me how to do the simple things a man should know how to do?" might be questions that have bred resentment in you.

Within most men lives a kind of paternal judgment, as though they know what it was like to walk in their father's shoes. To have carried the weight of his time, and his life, and his pain—to presume that faced with his father's decisions and circumstances, the son would have surely made better choices. In this way, many men live with the anger or pain of judging their father for not "fathering" them the way that they wanted. This is a grievance every man must heal and outgrow in order to embrace their own masculine maturity. Now, this anger and resentment may be a byproduct of the boy receiving harmful, incompetent, and wounding parenting from his father—all the more reason to prioritize understanding and healing.

Some boys may have grown up in a household where questioning the father was akin to questioning God. Or their father really was their idol and was an ideal man. Either way, they place their fathers on such a high pedestal that to see his flaws and imperfections is nearly impossible, and to attain the height his father achieved in his son's eyes is an equally insurmountable endeavor—leaving the man unable to grasp the fullness of his own power for fear of surpassing or confronting his idol.

Other boys will have been forced to eject from under their father's wing far too early after witnessing him become corrupt with power and authority—leaving the boy running from his own power, fearing his own potency and potential impact as he is in constant retreat from becoming anything like the man who brought him into the world.

Finally, like many modern men, perhaps you grew up with a meek, timid, and flaccid kind of man for a father whose vitality and assertiveness were nowhere to be found—only to come of age and discover it had been placed in the hands of your mother or stepmother. These fathers, who are largely conflict avoidant, lacking in direction and healthy boundaries, leave a heavy shadow for a boy to carry, tasking him with the confusing ordeal of having to sort out what it is to be a man with little to no guidance. These boys frequently lose respect and overpower their fathers at an early age, getting into conflict with their mothers, who take on the role of trying to quell the boy's teenage angst and aggression while the father sits idly by with a "go ask your mother" or "listen to your mother" motto.

THE PATERNAL PARADOX

This is the paradoxical role of a father—to be the example of presence, guidance, and security while covertly and overtly encouraging a boy to take risks, venture into the unknown, and explore the terrain of facing hardship. In this way, the father aids and guides the boy out of his adolescent comforts, specifically from the comforts and nurturing of his mother, and out into the dangers of the world.

To be a father is to exemplify what it looks like to have dominion over one's inner sanctum. To be the literal embodiment of positive masculine traits, values, and virtues so the boy can witness not only that they are required but also how they must be cultivated. To teach a boy that masculinity is not a given, nor will it be welcomed or fully wanted in some modern circles. Fathers play the vital role of showcasing what structure, order, discipline, and being a man of value can look like—the kind of man who has not only dedicated himself to the virtuous cause of crafting his own strengths and skills, but who has also learned how to bring his value to his family, community, and society. Without this positive example, a boy can enter into manhood lacking in direction, guidance, clarity, and the resiliency to pierce through the obstacles of his life.

Maybe you never knew your father and the absence left a masculine vacancy in your life. Maybe your father was an incredible man who was well loved by all, and you adopted a fear of never being able to develop into an equally impressive man. Perhaps your father was highly controlling and demanded perfection. Or maybe you grew up with a father who seriously lacked in any kind of masculine traits, direction, or vitality, causing you to resent him or constantly want more from him.

Regardless of what your dynamic was with your dad, the aim is not to blame him. Blaming is a way of escaping personal responsibility. What we are tasked with as men is to bring direct and radical honesty when exploring the impact our fathers had on our life, and to explore how we may still be living in his shadow so we can consciously and intentionally choose our own path forward.

The truth is that most fathers desire to raise sons who surpass them in some or all areas. And in order to do this, a son must be willing to heed the call of venturing far outside the territorial limits his father set (or failed to set) as a child. With this in mind, let's explore the elements of the father's shadow and how you can break free.

THE IMPACT OF ABSENT FATHERS

My parents divorced when I was three, and it fractured the time I got with my father. I remember countless nights for years afterward throwing tantrums, crying inconsolably, and raging against my mother because I wanted to be with my father. I couldn't understand what had happened. Why wasn't he around? Who the hell was the strange man in his place (my now stepfather), and what was I supposed to do with the vacancy my father's departure had left? It was a visceral kind of vacancy I had never experienced and didn't know how to cope with.

I got to see my dad every other weekend, but as he started his new family, I couldn't help but feel him moving further and further away. Now this isn't to slight him as a man or father in any way. He was and is a present, thoughtful, and loving man. However, as a boy, I didn't know how to deal with the pain of not having him around. Like most boys, I had a constant and seemingly insatiable appetite for time with my father, and the moments I got on weekends once or twice a month were admittedly insufficient for me. For some reason unknown to me, life had taken my father away and replaced him with some other man I vehemently rejected.

As I mentioned in a previous chapter, children are egocentric beings, and because I was in those formative years of attachment and bonding, my brain and body coded my father being gone as something wrong with *me*. Something I had done. Something I needed to fix. So, I did what most boys do in these situations: I acted out, rebelled, got into trouble at school, donned the robes of the class clown, fought with my stepfather constantly, and raised hell to make sure everyone knew I was less than happy about the circumstances. I was diagnosed with ADHD, put on medication, told I had learning and reading problems, and became the problem child who was unruly and wild. Thankfully my stepfather, while we never saw eye to eye when I was a kid, was a dedicated man who took on the daunting task of trying to create some form of discipline and order for me.

My parents' divorce would remain a mystery to me into my late twenties, but even as I entered into adulthood, I constantly found myself chasing after my father, trying to gain some kind of clarity about who he was so I could make sense of who I thought I needed to be in the world. It was as though he held the key to my liberation, freedom, and sovereignty as a man that I couldn't seem to acquire. Again, I didn't blame my father for his actions. In fact, once I had a better understanding of what had taken place, I understood why he decided to leave—but as I came to understand, *simply knowing why he left didn't change the impact of his leaving.*

My story is not unique. There are millions of iterations of this story, all with their own unique characters, arcs, and obstacles. The point here is this: *An absent father will always leave a vacancy in the heart, mind, and soul of the son.* It is a confronting truth for a man to come into contact with, whether he was the boy whose father was never around, the child who only got to see his father once in a while, or the boy whose father was around but who was emotionally, physically, and spiritually vacant. When a boy grows up without the warm, energizing presence of his father, it can feel like he has been restricted from receiving some vital form of psychological nutrition that he then tries to seek out in the world.

As James Hollis said, "Sons also need to watch their father in the world. They need him to show them how to be in the world, how to work, how to bounce back from adversity . . . They need the activation of their inherent masculinity both by outer modeling and by direct affirmation." The absence or inconsistency of this leaves a mark.

MAN OF THE HOUSE

Colin came downstairs from his bedroom to see what was going on. He heard yelling, and as a six-year-old boy he wanted to know what was going on. As he rounded the corner to the kitchen he could see his mother sitting at the kitchen table, tears streaming down her face, quickly trying to conceal that she was crying when she saw him appear.

Colin's father turned to see his son standing in his pajamas, curious about what was going on.

"Hi son, your mother and I are having a hard conversation, and I think it's time we talk to you as well," his father said, bending down to pick Colin up.

He sat Colin on his knee, reassured him that everything was going to be okay, and said, "I am going to be moving out of the house. I got a job in a different city, and your mother and I are going to be seeing each other less. Which means I will also be seeing you less. I want you to take good care of your mom. You're the man of the house now."

Colin was now a forty-three-year-old man with two kids and a wife he loved but struggled to connect with. He felt resentment and anger toward his wife for having to provide for the family. They had agreed that she would raise the kids and he would work, but a few years into it he found himself struggling to give them the quality of life he wanted and was constantly fighting with his wife about almost everything.

As we explored his past, Colin connected with the sadness of having his father leave, seeing the pain it caused his mother and the deep fear he had that he would be the cause of his own family's collapse. Colin began to realize how seriously he had taken his father's words. He had tried desperately as a child to take care of his mother while trying to get approval from his father. Colin had spent most of his childhood looking after his younger siblings, acting like their stand-in father, trying to be a good role model and discipline them when needed. He played intermediary between his parents and was tasked with passing on financial demands from his mom to his dad while having to set expectations with his mother when his father would not comply. When Colin's second child arrived he fell into a depression, became volatile around the home, and felt like his anger was completely out of control. He wasn't aware of it, but he was grieving the absence of his own childhood. He was bitter and angry and didn't know why, unable to see the impact of being thrust into the role of "man" far too soon.

When a father tells a child to be the man of the house, the child is immediately put in the position of being a failure, feeling constantly inadequate because he cannot possibly fulfill the roles and duties of the father. Even if the boy is never directly told to play this role, he can take up the added responsibility in an effort to fix, resolve, or make amends for the break in the household. This leads a boy to become a man who sets unattainable standards, goals, and expectations for himself. It is not merely that he believes he should be perfect, but rather that he believes he should be able to accomplish something he knows is impossible for him—continuing to engage in the shame of not being able to live up to the insurmountable expectations he took on as a child.

He is also left with the experience of being abandoned because he is no longer under the safe protection of his parents, but rather thrust into the caretaker role of one parent while being a subordinate to another who is not only severing his presence as a paternal figure, but also passing on his responsibilities to the child.

THE IMPACT

The *Palgrave Handbook of Male Psychology and Mental Health*, the single most comprehensive resource on male psychology, cites a father's absenteeism as having one of the most detrimental effects on a child's development, saying: "These outcomes (of lacking a father figure) are: ADHD, self-harm, and sexually inappropriate behavior." We can see this present in the rise of ADD, the fact that boys are much more likely to be diagnosed with ADD (12.9 percent of boys compared to 5.6 percent of girls), and that men on average are two to four times more likely to commit suicide than women.

The author of this section, Andrew Briggs, goes on to say: "By absent father I mean a father who may be physically present within the child's life but is psycho-emotionally or physically unavailable for his children. Whichever way he absents himself, or is made absent from the family, in itself has an impact upon his children's development."

Whether a father is absent because he is gone for weeks or months at a time at work, working twelve-hour shifts at his job, has limited custody after the divorce, or is emotionally and physically disengaged as a parent, the lack of male influence on boys has been deeply felt.

Fathers are also absent in a number of other ways—addictions to work, TV, alcohol, gambling, and distractions from social media can rip fathers away from their sons.

Now, in most myths and religions you see a father who is often absent on some form of adventure—living out his purpose, pursuing a mission, or modelling what it looks like to be a man deeply connected to what fuels and fulfills him. There is deep value in this as it can teach a young boy what it means to be a man connected to purpose; however, this is not the reality most boys grew up witnessing. Watching your father come home after a twelve-hour day at a job he genuinely hates only to sit on the couch drinking beer and mindlessly watching TV before going to bed and repeating the cycle isn't exactly the story that legends and myths are built upon.

Outside of these obvious versions of absent fathers are the male parents who are deeply disconnected from their own masculinity and have adopted a female-centric version of what a father should look like. These men are often immature, avoid responsibility, and likely didn't grow up with men around or were told that men were dangerous. Because of this, they outsource and defer most parenting and relationship decisions to the mother, playing a ghostlike role of a father. These men lack opinions, direction, assertiveness, and fail to create any kind of structure or order for their children—leaving their sons malnourished in healthy, positive masculinity.

The role of the father is an integral one to a child's development, especially to the development of young boys as they largely learn how to regulate their systems through interaction with their fathers, as shown in some of the latest research. In a recent article Allan Schore demonstrates that between eighteen and twenty-four months fathers play a fundamental role in regulating the aggression of their children of both sexes. Rough and tumble play between many fathers and their children especially helps boy toddlers control their testosterone-induced aggression, through imprinting their left brains. This aspect of the role of fathers allows for their children to develop into self-regulated young people in society.

As a result of growing up with absent fathers, countless men will struggle to effectively regulate and lead themselves. They may appear to have it together from the outside but will have a deep sense of lacking direction while feeling incapable of creating the change they ultimately want.

Symptoms of men with absent fathers include:

— Prioritizing other people's needs above their own

— Repressed or volatile anger and aggression

— Disconnection from masculine energy and traits

— Fear of, or challenge connecting to, other men

— Remaining in unsatisfying relationships or careers

— Lacking self-leadership and direction

— Feeling out of control physically, mentally, sexually, or emotionally

— Seeking approval from others, especially women who have largely raised them

Now, just because there are challenges that come along with having been raised with an absent father doesn't mean you are doomed to dysfunction. And if your father wasn't around in the way you wanted him to be, this doesn't mean he was a deadbeat or is to blame for all of your problems as a man. What it means is that you are honest about the role he played in your life so you can exit from the childish position of wanting him to change, show up in the way you want, or be different.

Part of a man's work is to learn how to activate and cultivate within what he did not receive from outside himself. Said another way: a man must be willing to cultivate the skills, virtues, and attributes he wanted his father to exude or teach him. The coming chapters will give you tools to do exactly that.

UNDERSTANDING YOUR FATHER'S PAIN

Every man will be faced with the inevitable task of sifting through the masculine hand-me-downs of his father's pain: the father's shame about having lived a dramatically unsatisfying life, disconnected and hidden anger, or abuse and trauma from generations past left unhealed, flowing through the father and into the son. A father's pain, if left unattended, will inevitably become the burden of the son.

In his book *Finding Our Fathers*, Samuel Osherson cites an in-depth yet shocking study in which only 17 percent of American men reported having a positive relationship with their father during their youth. This means that, on average, eighty-three out of one hundred boys will have had an unsatisfying or negative relationship with their father. Even if the reality isn't as harsh as this study reports, it still points to the fact that something tragic has happened to one of the most important roles in a boy's life, causing a serious imbalance.

For some boys, their father's pain will have been a distant yet palpable presence occupying the space between the father they dreamt about having and the father they got. They will have grown up with the ever-present feeling that they know only half of the man who raised them. Countless questions about who their father is and what he was like in his youth, as well as a kind of vacancy, will occupy a man's perspective of his father.

Tim felt this way about his dad. They got along well and were able to spend time together often when he was a boy and teenager. His dad would take him to baseball practice and coach his little league team, but as Tim got older and moved out of the house, he began to realize that he didn't really have a clue about who his father was. While his dad was around he usually seemed distant, almost as if he was somewhere else entirely.

When Tim would ask his father about his childhood, he would deflect away from the conversation, saying something like, "Those days are in the past. I don't like to think about them anymore." Tim's father was a serious man who rarely opened up, and Tim frequently found himself wondering what had happened. Tim's grandfather was a World War II veteran and an even harder man. He said very little, had no time for small talk, and had steely blue eyes that still seemed to carry the weight of the war. Tim's father never spoke of his childhood or shared any feelings about his own parents, but he would be agitated for days and sometimes weeks after interacting with them.

Even in his early forties, Tim found himself deeply angry with his father for being such a distant man. Tim had never been able to break through, and now that his father was at the end of his life, having been diagnosed with Parkinson's disease, Tim had become resentful of him for spending his whole life unable to talk about his past, which created a canyon between father and son.

For other men, their father's or stepfather's pain will have been the main source of connection. Boys who grow up around fathers with loud, explosive anger learn quickly that the best way to gain Dad's attention is by acting out, shutting down, or conforming to Dad's expectations without question. These boys unconsciously see their father's pain as the main access point to getting love, sometimes making it their personal mission to fix the pain by shape-shifting into whatever their father needs, mirroring their father's aggression, or completely disconnecting from their own anger in an attempt to "never be like him."

For some boys, their father's pain will have been packed deeply like tobacco in the lower chambers of their heart, a feeling the boys will one day know all too well, though they'll be perplexed about its origin. These men grow up around soft, confused, and overly domesticated men who have chosen the path of disassociating from their own anger, heat, and hurt. These fathers were crippled by their pain, often amputating their assertiveness, drive, and direction, usually choosing overly dominant women who told them how to live. This leaves the boy scrambling as he crosses the threshold of puberty, finding himself alone as he enters manhood.

Whatever the response from the boy, the main relationship he has is not with his father but with his father's pain, shame, anger, and aggression.

As John Bradshaw, a well-known counsellor and author of the book *Healing the Shame That Binds You,* said, "Pass it back or pass it on." The idea here is simple: either you gain awareness of what you have been given so you can make a clear, sovereign choice about what to do with it, or you remain ignorant to it and pass it on through your lineage, relationships, and community.

Let's look at your father's pain and how it may have impacted your life.

QUESTIONS TO ANSWER ▸ TRUTHS TO UNCOVER

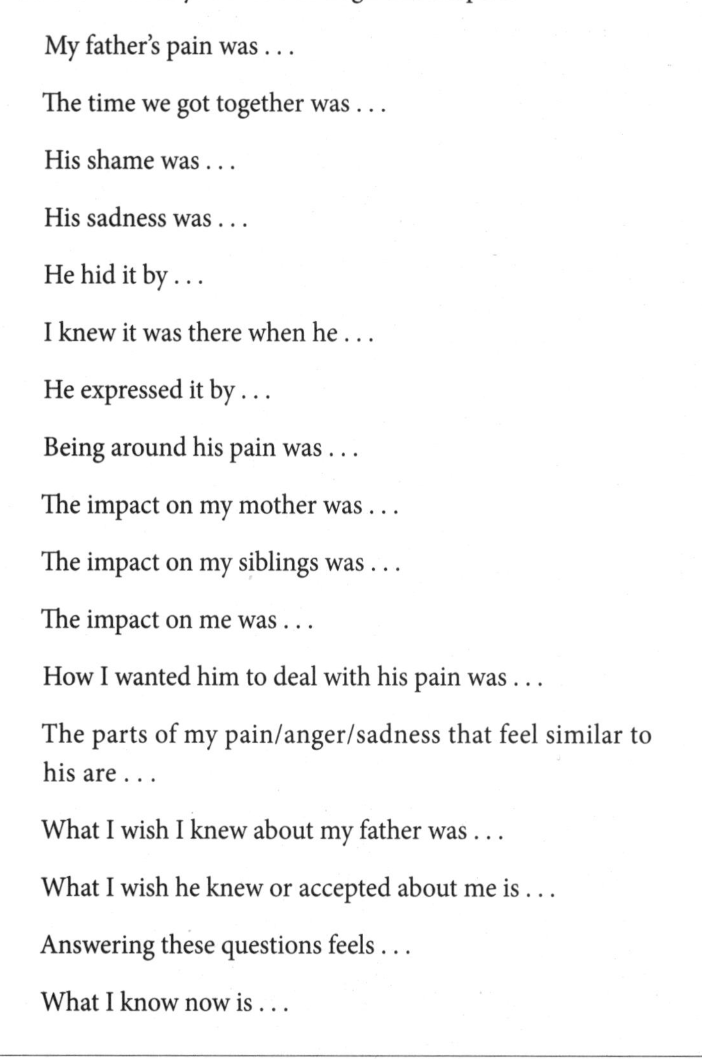

Answer the questions below and expand on them as much as you'd like. Some of the questions below can be journaling prompts you use this week as you move through this chapter.

My father's pain was . . .

The time we got together was . . .

His shame was . . .

His sadness was . . .

He hid it by . . .

I knew it was there when he . . .

He expressed it by . . .

Being around his pain was . . .

The impact on my mother was . . .

The impact on my siblings was . . .

The impact on me was . . .

How I wanted him to deal with his pain was . . .

The parts of my pain/anger/sadness that feel similar to his are . . .

What I wish I knew about my father was . . .

What I wish he knew or accepted about me is . . .

Answering these questions feels . . .

What I know now is . . .

YOUR FATHER'S ANGER

A man's relationship to his own anger can be understood through his father's anger. A man's ability to regulate his nervous system and emotions can also be understood through his father's ability to regulate himself. This is true until a man liberates himself from the automatic reaction he developed in the absence or presence of his father's anger—and if he doesn't, Dad is still in control.

This isn't to say that your father is *responsible* for how you act as a man or is to blame for your behavior, anger, or ability to regulate—that's your responsibility. However, learning to see your father more accurately is imperative in building and embracing your own sovereignty and autonomy.

One of the primary functions a father plays in a boy's life is to help teach a boy how to regulate himself and provide order within his life, body, and mind. This is especially true when a boy crosses the threshold into puberty and his body undergoes the dramatic change of producing more and more testosterone, leading to more volatility, sexual urges, and an often deep desire to test authority and limitations.

A father's ability to regulate his own nervous system and anger response will be the baseline example of how a boy learns to regulate himself and defines what girls will come to expect from men.

Imagine your father getting angry. Why he is angry is less relevant for this exercise; simply imagine him fully engulfed in his own anger. What comes to mind? Is this your normal experience of him? Are these the moments that often come to mind when you think of him? Did you see and hear his anger directly, or is it hidden behind gritted teeth and passive comments? Do you struggle to conjure up any image of this, having never really seen it?

What about your body—how does it respond to your father's anger? Does it want to run and hide? Cower and cave in? Do you feel small and constricted at the thought of being around his anger? Or do you feel heat rising up in your chest, arms ready for action and feet wanting to move? Maybe you feel numb, nothing, or empty, unable to connect to a real physical response.

And what about your behaviors? How did you have to act, behave, or react when his anger was present? What was it like for you and your family to be around, and how did you compensate? How did you act, behave, or react when his anger wasn't there or couldn't be evoked? Did you act out and shit test him to see where the boundaries were?

Growing up, I found myself in between the anger of two very different men. My biological father rarely got angry. I could tell when he was upset and largely wouldn't do anything to illicit his anger as I idolized him and didn't want to squander the time I got to spend with him. Small things would sometimes bother him, and I can remember crusadelike campaigns and brief rants against things he was upset by—the war on the ants in the garage, something the neighbors at the lake had said over the weekend, and a general deep frustration toward people he deemed incompetent. For the most part, my father's anger was managed, maybe buried at times, but never threatening or dangerous.

My stepfather was a different beast. He had a short temper, was loud, and wasn't afraid to let it loose. His ability to regulate his own anger was often limited, and so I adopted his short fuse and sometimes volatile reactivity. He and I locked horns constantly, getting into loud arguments that came very close to physical blows on multiple occasions as I got older. As a child I resented him and viewed him as being one of the main reasons my parents were divorced. This was not true at all, but I made sure he knew on an almost daily basis that I did not approve of him. I'd challenge his every decision, reject and ignore his direction, and even went so far as to steal from him—sometimes even taking his car for joy rides with my friends at the age of thirteen, something I'm sure he'll enjoy reading in this book. Much of my childhood was spent in defiance of this man who was doing his very best to raise me as his own. Nothing like having a feral child in your home, constantly trying to provoke you.

Both of these men taught me a great deal about anger. On the one hand I saw a man whose anger could be explosive, loud, outwardly directed, and volatile, while the other was docile, steadfast, and largely didn't show much anger at all.

What I witnessed and learned was that anger could either be explosive, outwardly directed, or implosive, inwardly directed—neither of which taught me how to truly regulate my own inner realm (something we will cover in depth in later chapters).

As I grew older, I found myself distancing myself from my anger as I believed it was dangerous and potentially harmful, a byproduct of having pedestaled my father's absence of anger and going to war with the volatility of my stepfather's. I found myself having fewer outlets for my own anger as a young adult and would channel it into all-night benders and bar fights—something I actively looked forward to and would have as my primary focus when going out with "the boys" some weekends.

Drink—get fucked up—fuck someone up—find a woman—take her home. This was the pattern I used to deal with my inner rage. I would be calm and charismatic most of the time, getting along with almost anyone I met while repressing any anger I had, only to let it erupt under certain conditions.

Again, neither of my fathers' anger was good or bad. It's not about having a father who "got it right" so much as it is necessary for a son to accept and learn from what he observed. My stepfather's anger and heat helped to keep me in check while my biological father's calm and compassionate manner showed me a different path. Both were equally valuable.

I'm like many men in that the anger I saw in my father (or fathers, in my case) imprinted itself deeply in the architectural blueprint of my psyche. It was the program running in the background of my behavior, shaping the way I regulated my mind and body until I learned to choose a different path besides just opposing or repeating my father's anger.

In order to choose a different path, I needed to explore the reality and impact of the anger I'd witnessed from both of my fathers so I could not only see the impact it had on my life, but choose a different, more integrated, sovereign path for myself.

This is a pivotal part of a man's work—being able to understand how your father's anger and ability to regulate shaped your own relationship to anger. We will explore your anger more in later chapters and how to work with it, but in the meantime, dive into the questions and exercise below to have a better understanding of your father's anger, its impact, and how you responded.

QUESTIONS TO ANSWER ▸ TRUTHS TO UNCOVER

In this section, explore the nuances and depths of your father's anger.

My father's anger was . . .

It showed up when . . .

It was hidden when . . .

The impact it had on my mother was . . .

The impact it had on my family/siblings was . . .

Being around it felt . . .

I tried to avoid it by . . .

I tried to evoke his anger by . . .

What I always wanted to say to my father about his anger was . . .

Now let's look at your anger.

How I express my anger today is . . .

If my father saw me expressing my anger like this, he would . . .

Knowing the above feels . . .

INTEGRATION EXERCISE

Write a letter to your father, or directly to his anger (you are *not* going to send it to him or show him).

Be as detailed as you want, describing what it was like for you as a boy to be around his anger. What did it teach you? What have you come to appreciate about his anger? What have you still not forgiven him for when he was caught in his anger? What do you wish he *would have* done if he was better at expressing his anger?

When you're ready, share this letter with a man in your life or a men's group you are a part of, letting yourself feel the full weight of it as you read it aloud.

OPPOSING VS. REPEATING THE WAY OF THE FATHER

Free yourself from living in opposition to or repetition of your father.

Say your father was a loud, obtuse, and sometimes violent man. The shadow he cast was that of being ignorant to the suffering and pain he inflicted on others. You saw the impacts of his ignorance and aggression, and as a result you work diligently to be nothing like him. You overemphasize the qualities of your personality that are more agreeable, nice, and make sure to always place a high value on other people's feelings, needs, and perspectives so you never make them feel the way you did.

However, living in this way has created its own blindness. Notice what you have had to cut yourself off from in order to *not be like him.* You are likely cut off from your anger, lack assertiveness, and have found yourself resentful of and judgmental toward those who are openly direct and speak their needs. Your relationship likely suffers the consequence of this as you withhold your needs or disconnect from your anger, tightly suppressing what needs to be expressed externally.

Repeating the way of your father is likely no better, and it's usually less obvious.

James found himself next in line to take over the family business. He was the oldest of three, married, and had four children of his own. He had worked with his father for several years after leaving his career in finance and was a few years away from taking over the marketing company his father had spent his life building. He wanted to make his father proud and had been doing everything in his power to learn and emulate his father's leadership style.

James had come to work with me because he had been having an affair with one of the women in the office and was completely lost as to why the affair had begun. As we explored his infidelity, James revealed the pressure he felt growing up to conform to his father's expectations. He idolized his father and had largely been a good kid throughout his childhood, making sure to meet his father's expectations and do his best to walk in his father's shoes.

"I don't get it!" he would say about the affair. "I just don't get why I would do this at work of all places. If my dad found out about this he would be furious."

We explored the affair, the thrill of workplace sexual encounters in bathrooms and locked offices. James described how freeing it was to have this secret affair and how powerful he felt when the encounters would happen, followed by the shame that would set in after.

"We would finish and I'd walk back to my office. Sometimes straight into a meeting with the board and my father. On one hand I felt disgusted by my actions, and on the other it was exhilarating. It was like I was going against everything I had been working so hard to build, which was the most confusing part," James disclosed in one of our sessions.

After one exercise in which James imagined confronting his father about the affair, he realized that he had never rebelled against his dad and that most of his life was controlled, orchestrated, and determined by his father. The affair was a way to break free of repeating his father's expectations, carving out some form of his own path, albeit an unconscious one.

Liberating yourself from living in opposition to or repetition of your father is essential. Look at the ways you've tried not to be like him. What's the price you've paid? How has this kept you restricted or bound to him? What have you repeated? What about your father are you still trying to understand, following blindly in his footsteps? Be honest with yourself and inquire with people who know you both. Maybe your wife or sibling can shed light on how you are repeating your father's behaviors and choices or allude to how you seem to be living in opposition of him.

Here are two steps you can take to begin liberating yourself from your father:

1) Spend one whole day this week living as if your father had the most significant impact on your life, and see whether your actions and behaviors are in accordance with or in defiance of him. Where are you falling in line with what he would have expected from you, or acting in direct opposition to him? Take notes or journal about the experience.

2) Sit down with a man you trust, or a men's group you are a part of, and talk about your father and your relationship to him for a minimum of twenty minutes. Do this intentionally, describing what he was like, your judgments of him, betrayals, and anything you wished he had given or taught you. Once you're done, ask the men for their feedback and observations about how you may be living in repetition of or opposition to your father.

LEARN HOW TO FATHER YOURSELF

In Norse mythology there is a being who represents the eternal embodiment of the father and who is arguably one of the most complex characters in all of mythology. He is known as the Master of Ecstasy, the God of wisdom, Allfather, father of men, father of the age, father of war, victory, and The Furious. This archetypal father, who was the father of the Gods, has been the epitome of the masculine spirit for thousands of years. In many ways, he is the representation of how a boy sees his father—a God among men.

Odin, or his old Norse name *Óðinn*, is formed from two parts: first, the noun *óðr*, "ecstasy, fury, inspiration," and the suffix *-inn*, the masculine definite article, which, when added to the end of a word like this, means something like "the master of" or "a perfect example of."

Surprisingly, Master of Ecstasy is not likely what one would think of when describing the archetypal father figure. However, this form of ecstasy is the precise reason why this word is used. Odin's life and story, indeed the ecstasy he represented, were a reminder of the unifying forces behind the countless areas of life he was associated with: sovereignty, wisdom, magic, war, poetry, shamanism, and the dead.

Odin is also many things, a multidimensional man—a savage, a shaman, a wise old man, the father of Gods, keeper of magic, speaker of poetry, and presider over the dead. He is, in essence, a kind of Nietzschean *Ubermensch* in God form. He embodies the many dimensions, pursuits, desires, and traits of the masculine psyche—a manifestation of the eternal father who relentlessly ventures outward into the universe seeking to satiate his internal hungers, both for his own pleasure and for the betterment of the space he inhabits.

One of the pivotal moments or stories in the Odin lore is his discovery of, and journey into, the depths of the Runes. In the Norse cosmos, Asgard—which is known as the realm of the Gods—rests in the upper branches of Yggdrasil, an immense and sacred tree surrounded by all of existence, including the Nine Worlds. To access the wisdom within the Runes, Odin knew he would be forced to make a sacrifice, to endure a shamanic initiation of sorts where he would be faced with the task of proving himself worthy of the terrifying wisdom and abilities that the Runes held.

So, Odin set himself to the task. He hung himself from a branch of Yggdrasil, pierced himself with his spear, and peered downward into the shadowy waters below. He demanded that no other God interfere as his trials were his and his alone, knowing surely that the wisdom would not be granted to him if he was aided by others. He stared downward, and stared downward, and called to the Runes. He lingered in this state for nine days and nights, teetering on the brink of insanity, pushing his mind and body past its limitations. At the end of the ninth night, he at last perceived shapes in the depths: the Runes had been revealed.

The Runes had accepted his sacrifice, revealing themselves and their forms to him along with the secrets that lie within them. Odin soaked up their wisdom and committed it to his memory, imprinting it into his being—elevating himself as a God and doing something no other dared.

With the knowledge he acquired from his trials, he learned how to wield the power of the Runes. Because of this trial he became one of the most accomplished, powerful, and revered beings in the cosmos. He learned skills to free himself from constraints, tactics to ward off and vanquish practitioners of evil magic, and chants to heal emotional and physical wounds. He learned the secrets of how to win and keep a lover and protect his allies in battle and garnered the ability to wake the dead.

And while these things are wonderfully symbolic, the tale is less about the outcome. This particular story is not about what Odin gained as a result of his initiatory test, but rather one that codifies an incredibly important message for men: *sacrifice yourself to yourself.*

Odin's story is the antidote to Henry David Thoreau's sentiment that "most men lead lives of quiet desperation and go to the grave with the song still in them."

Odin's story is a myth that delivers the cure for a man's boredom and reminds us that we have a deep craving for adventure, challenge, and knowledge.

Odin shows us that we have to sacrifice a part of ourselves to ourselves to receive the wisdom of the Runes—the wisdom of the depths and the unknown. In order to access the song within himself, Odin had to sacrifice his "lower self" to his "higher self," putting aside his ego, power, cunning, and physical prowess and surrendering fully to his higher self—the divine-oriented self who wanted wisdom to be a more complete leader, healer, poet, father, and man. And you must be willing to do the same.

There are two parts to learning how to father yourself. The first aim is the same as Odin's—*to learn how to sacrifice yourself to yourself.* To learn how to sacrifice the youthful ignorance and Peter Pan behaviors to the elder within. To learn how to sacrifice the lazy, unmotivated, sabotaging, risk-avoidant, self-deprecating, disbelieving version of yourself to the new, more potent and capable version.

Now, obviously this doesn't warrant enduring the kind of physical harm Odin did, although there is merit in undertaking experiences like vision quests and rituals that may test your limits physically, mentally, emotionally, and spiritually. To learn how to sacrifice your lesser qualities will likely put you into direct contact with the ways in which you are already harming yourself and holding yourself back. To set yourself ferociously to the task of not only relinquishing your lowly behaviors—like the unhealthy eating, infidelity, or constant negative self-talk—but also to developing the skills, attributes, and qualities you know you need to be a more robust man.

And this may require hardship. It may require that you get wildly uncomfortable, whether this means you must confront your own ego and find a mentor who can point you in the right direction, wander off into the forest for several days alone, fast, decide to give up drinking alcohol, or stop watching your precious TV shows. It may mean enrolling yourself in martial arts so you can develop the physical confidence you've been lacking for decades, learning survival skills, or developing the habit of waking up at a certain time and building a more generative morning routine. It may mean that you enroll in some form of continuing education, embark on a spiritual quest, or do stand-up comedy on the weekends because you've wanted to develop the ability to speak truth through the medium of humor.

Regardless of the endeavor, fathering yourself will require that you actively develop and sacrifice your lesser self—the beliefs, fears, insecurities, and weaknesses—to your higher self. To aim, as Odin did, at "mastering" your own ecstasy, fury, and inspiration. To seek and be the embodiment of wisdom in whatever aspects of life you deem to be meaningful. To grow deeper into yourself, your capabilities, and your competence as a man.

The second aim is to learn how to father the boy within you. The boy who didn't receive guidance from Dad or was abused by him and doesn't trust men; who didn't get empathy or compassion from Mom and now seeks that validation from women; who felt neglected, outcast, or chronically alone and now doesn't know how to develop deep relationships as an adult. Maybe the boy in you was bullied and became a scared man who doesn't know how to stand up for himself, or the boy was never shown how to learn, train his body, or interact with women. This boy needs you to step in and develop the competence and skills he never received. The key word here being *competence*, whether in self-direction, discipline, compassion, emotional regulation, self-recognition, or any other valuable trait that would help take the boy in you out of the driver's seat.

I remember the moment when I finally understood the importance of this work. The concept of needing to "father myself" felt annoying, vague, and somewhat ridiculous. What purpose or relevance did my childhood have, and what good would fathering myself do? I found myself not wanting to even think about my childhood—until one day, visiting my parents in my childhood home, I came across a photo of myself when I was about five years old. In the photo I was sitting in a giant cooking pot full of hot water and soap on the back deck, apparently taking a bath. I had a Band-Aid across my knee, was covered in dirt, and had the biggest grin on my face—the kind you have when the weight of the world and reality haven't sunken deep into your bones. As I looked at that boy, I felt the heaviness of all the years that stood between the two of us. All the hurt I had endured, the terrible decisions I had made, and the anger I had been carrying. I felt the weight of grief wash over me as I realized I had been a terrible steward to that boy. I hadn't become a man the boy in me could trust or even respect. The boy certainly didn't trust me as a man, and I knew that as a fact because *I didn't trust myself as a man*. I hadn't become a man who could truly let that boy rest. So, he was still in charge.

I had let the boy remain in charge of too many things: relationships, money, career, discipline—all were being dictated by the boy in some way.

I could finally see the disorderly, juvenile state of my life for what it was—a life built by a boy, not a man. I started to see it in the way I would reject responsibility in an argument, in how I did not take ownership over my failures, in the risks I was hiding from, in the constant and incessant validation I hungered for from women, and in all the hard conversations I had been avoiding. I had to develop discipline, face the truths I had been avoiding, repair my relationships with other men, and undertake countless other endeavors.

Over the years, I've seen this to be the case with many men, even into their fifties and sixties. Men who feel brutally ill-equipped to deal with the responsibilities of their lives don't feel like men internally. They constantly long for an escape from the life they lead and turn away from the harshness of reality.

Look at your childhood and connect to the boy within. What does he lack? What does he need, specifically from his father? Does he need guidance? Mentorship? Encouragement to take risks or pursue his interests? Does the boy in you need more love and validation? Does he crave to be held or taught basic survival skills? Maybe the boy in you needs to be pushed and challenged, or have Dad stand up to Mom, or give protection from an abusive family member, or confront his own demons, or simply be more present. Where in your life, if you're brutally honest, are you still acting like a child—rejecting responsibility, acting helpless, and avoiding action when you know what is needed from you? These are the things you will need to discover to gain clarity on what it looks like to father yourself and take the inner child within out of the driver's seat of your life.

Become the man your younger self needed. Become the man the boy wants to look up to, learn from, and aspire to be and surpass. The result of this work calls you forward into a more mature version of yourself. It allows you to stop acting like a child in your relationship, health, finances, or career and helps you develop the skills and competency you have always craved.

QUESTIONS TO ANSWER ▸ TRUTHS TO UNCOVER

As you are reflecting on how to father yourself, spend some time completing each statement below.

What I wanted my father to teach me as a boy was . . .

When I think about myself as a boy, I feel . . .

As a child, what I needed most from my father that I didn't get was . . .

What my father gave me that was invaluable was . . .

If I had the perfect male role model, what I'd want to learn from him is . . .

The one skill or trait I've always wanted to develop is . . .

Where I still act out of control, petulant, or like a child is . . .

The skills I want to develop are . . .

The one passion I've wanted to pursue more actively is . . .

INTEGRATION EXERCISE

Based on your answers to the statements above, make a list of all the aspects of life you wish your father had taught you, or the things the boy in you needed to become a man. Choose one to focus on for the next thirty days and immerse yourself in that skill. This could be a disciplined morning routine, hiring a trainer to work out with two or three times per week, a coach to improve your mindset, archery, woodworking, financial literacy, etc. It might mean committing to a practice of taking risks, learning self-protection, becoming financially literate, or anything the boy in you needs to release control.

Finally, write a letter to your father and create a ceremony to release him. You may write the letter and read it out to your men's group before burning it, or read the letter when out hiking in the deep woods before burying it. Regardless, the letter is not for your father or to be sent to him, but it should cover two important elements:

1) Everything he did and didn't do that you've held resentment, pain, bitterness, or sadness for, making it clear what exactly you wanted/needed.

2) Forgiving and releasing him entirely from being at fault for the man you are today. Reclaim your sovereignty and make it clear that you are in charge of developing yourself into the man you wish to be. Declare how you will love him and honor him moving forward as a son.

CHAPTER 4

KNOW YOUR PAIN

"Our wounds are the doorway to rediscovering our true nature."

PAUL LEVY

MOST OF MY adult life was spent trying to avoid, deny, reject, numb out, or eradicate the pain I felt. I didn't want to know my pain because it seemed monumental and too much to handle, whether it was grief from my childhood, heartbreak from relationships, rejection, embarrassment, boredom, loneliness, or the existential weight of trying to figure out what the hell to do with my life. I had built an entire identity around avoiding the emotional and psychological things I didn't want to deal with.

Looking back now, I can honestly say I was never really taught as a boy or as a man what to do when I was hurting. Most of the advice I got sounded something like, "Just be more vulnerable," or "Drink it off, get laid, stop thinking about it, work harder, or jerk off and you'll feel better." And so, I did. I tried all the prescribed and acceptable methods that we as men tell one another in modern culture. I drank, smoked, screwed, worked, earned, gamed, and numbed it all away. Or so I thought. As time went on, I needed stronger numbing agents. More porn, more booze, more social media, more women and more distraction. I was, in most aspects of my life, numb.

To be clear, the pain wasn't the problem. How I was trying to deal with it was the real issue. Pain, as I've come to learn, is either a teacher and guide for us as men, or our owner.

Maybe you've caught yourself numbing out and avoiding your pain and suffering. Maybe you numb out a lot, even daily. You don't want to feel the grief or sadness from a breakup, want to avoid your own confusion about a relationship or work situation, or simply want to tune out the negative thoughts, worries, and doubts bombarding your mind and inner dialogue—so you turn on the TV, swipe through a dating app, watch porn, light a joint, or have a drink.

Pain ignored. Suffering subsided. Mission accomplished.

But here's the catch: you numb out not because you are emotionally empty, but because you are emotionally full. Your body and mind have reached their limit of stress, anger, anxiousness, boredom, or loneliness and need to escape.

Numbness is not necessarily a bad thing—it is a merely a sign that the shadow is present. When you engage in numbing behaviors, it's likely because you are feeling something you can't avoid any longer—a pain, sadness, rage, frustration, disappointment, or grief that demands your attention.

But when you ignore the pain, you also ignore the wisdom and intelligence your pain has to offer. As Francis Weller, a renowned American therapist, says, "Your pain has its own intelligence." You can either learn to listen to the intelligence of your pain or be subjected to its will and wants. Sabotage, for example, is the intelligence of your pain thwarting the goals and direction you have consciously laid out for yourself.

Ignored pain becomes the driving force behind a man's decline and descent into the abyss of rock bottom. Queue the image of my 6'2" frame crammed into the back of a 2005 Pontiac G5 with hideous chrome rims, double racing stripes, and an oversized (and practically pointless) fin bolted to the trunk, and you'll see the picture of a man who ignored his pain—only to be outwitted by its intelligence.

TURNING PAIN INTO PURPOSE

Do not aim to eliminate or avoid your pain. Instead learn to understand it and carry it more effectively. In this way, you give your pain a purpose in your life. You invite the dragon—your pain—to take a seat at the table rather than pretending it doesn't exist or needs to be killed off.

Unfortunately, some men, like myself, get tricked into believing the only way change will happen—the only way we can break free from bad habits, lies, and sabotage—is to bottom out. As if having everything crumble and die away is both the punishment we deserve and the salvation we seek. This is the illusion we must confront before we can take the first step on the path toward purpose—to pull ourselves from the nihilistic perspective that pain is meaningless.

The challenge most will face is that it's easier to say *fuck you* than to say *I am hurt.* But this is exactly what you must do—know unequivocally where you are hurting and be able to admit it, at least to yourself.

If you feel like you lack purpose, or a foundation of meaning in life, and you don't know where to find it, the first place you can and should begin is with your suffering. What would it look like for you to heal your constant anger, face your overwhelming stress and anxiety, or confront the insecurities you've been trying to cover up for years? You may be carrying the pain of not feeling smart enough and pick up a second language as a means of pushing your edge. Or you might feel a deep insecurity of not being good enough for the woman you're with or the women you date. What is the wisdom of your insecurity trying to teach you? Do you worry about not being good enough in the bedroom? Maybe you should pick up a few books about sexual skills, take a course, or sign up for a workshop to better learn how to work with your own sexual arousal and energy. Most things, sexual prowess included, are skills you can acquire, deepen, sharpen, and expand over time, so long as you are committed.

The key here is that your pain is pointing you in a direction. The direction of healing. And that direction is almost always a deeply meaningful path. It illuminates what needs to be forgiven, accepted, or developed. It will ask you to expand your capacities, capabilities, physical conditioning, and psychological strength.

Pain points to where you feel a deep sense of lack and shows you what action can be taken to grow or heal.

Maybe your path is like mine—wild, out of control, deeply ashamed of who you are, and lacking discipline. My pain was practically pleading with me to develop self-reliance, forgive the people who I felt betrayed by as a boy, and unapologetically own the kind of life, relationship, and man I knew I could create.

Begin by asking these simple questions: "What is my pain trying to teach me? What is it asking me to do, develop, learn, forgive, or become?" Maybe you need to admit that you drink a little too much to cover up how unhappy you are in your marriage or job. Maybe your pain is asking you to forgive yourself for decisions you made in the past, or to commit to developing a deeper sense of self-reliance. Your pain might be asking you to have an incredibly challenging conversation to forgive someone who betrayed you, or to get yourself into shape after letting years of bullying rip apart your self-image. Or your pain might need you to take the first step of admitting that not having your father in your life was more damaging and painful than you've let yourself see.

Regardless of what it reveals, shifting your narrative that pain is useless, meaningless, or should just "go away" is a noble first step. Then, being open to the possibility that your pain can sharpen you as a man, can expand who you are at your core, is the second act.

The truth about pain and suffering is that it's usually asking you to build yourself into the kind of man who knows how to respond when suffering comes knocking. A man who knows he can navigate through hardship is a man who has immense value to himself, his family, community, and the world.

Suffering is inevitable, but your ability to alchemize pain is not automatically granted. It must be earned. You must fight through the fear—and the resistance that is sure to follow.

WORK WITH THE RESISTANCE

The key to all of this resides in your ability to face and move through resistance. If you've ever tried to start a new habit, you'll know exactly what I'm talking about. I remember trying to create a morning routine for myself—getting up at 6:00 a.m., stretching, writing, breathwork.

It was an incredible challenge, and I faced a massive amount of resistance. Each morning my alarm would go off and every cell in my body would be saying, "Hell no! Not yet. Just hit snooze." The resistance I felt to becoming the disciplined, structured, and competent man my pain was asking me to become was real and intense.

Resistance is the main challenge we face when trying to heal, create change, or step into our power. Many men code or label their resistance as something that "shouldn't be happening," as bad, wrong, or a sign they are moving in the wrong direction.

But resistance isn't bad. Resistance is simply a strategy or mechanism designed to protect you and keep you safe.

The strange thing about this mechanism is that it sometimes tries to "protect" you from things you know are good for you—like going to the gym, starting a healthy routine, or pursuing the relationship you know is good for you.

For example, say you grew up in a household where conflict was volatile and sometimes dangerous. Maybe your father's anger was loud and chaotic. Because of this, you've built resistance toward having confronting conversations and have disconnected from your own anger—thus disconnecting from your assertiveness. You've developed a fear of anger and confrontation, both in yourself and your partner. When an argument or disagreement happens, your partner might get heated and animated, something that may feel like your father's anger. Deep down you want to be able to communicate in those moments, but the resistance you experience tells you that "This shouldn't be happening" or "They shouldn't be acting like this" or "What the hell is wrong with me? Why can't I speak up for myself?" You shut down, disconnect, and turn to your favorite numbing agent—porn, social media, video games, work, booze, etc. Here, the experience of growing up in a hostile environment has translated into a behavior of disconnecting from your anger and disengaging when your partner is angry as a means of *protecting* everyone involved. What's required of you to turn this pain into purpose is to learn to engage in the conflict in a healthy way—staying grounded, connecting to your breath, communicating boundaries, listening intently, and being assertive when needed.

Resistance will either be the thing that sends you back to old patterns and behaviors aimed at avoiding your pain or the doorway you walk through to meet your edge, take new action, and expand—connecting you to purpose and meaning.

Your masculine core and confidence will gain strength and reinforcement as you allow your resistance to be a guide rather than an obstacle. In fact, your masculine core craves this and has a deep desire to meet your resistance. Think about where you're feeling resistance in your life right now. Maybe you need to have a conversation with your partner or boss that you have been dreading. When you avoid this conversation and cave into the resistance, you feel weak and insecure, and shame begins to set in. However, when you consciously choose to confront it and engage with it, you feel alive, emboldened, and meet an edge you would have normally shrunk from. By staying engaged, you build confidence, resilience, and trust.

The more you question your resistance and look for opportunities to work with it or push through it, the more you will meet your natural edge. Your physical or emotional edge—your edge in communication, relationships, intimacy, abundance, and sex—shows up when you move toward your resistance. It is not something you can ignore, break, or beat into submission.

This is an essential and important element to being a self-led man: to discern when you are protecting yourself unnecessarily from resistance and need to move forward or have reached a limit and need to rest. Resistance leads you to your edge, and your capacity to play, operate, and meet this edge is what creates expansion. Expansion is essential because it is the energy of purpose. The more you are willing to press yourself against and through the natural resistance you feel, the more you will know where your edge lives, and the more expansion you will generate.

Spend time with your resistance and notice the natural expansion, edge, and limits it is guiding you toward. Start today by taking action on the questions and exercises below.

QUESTIONS TO ANSWER ▸ TRUTHS TO UNCOVER

Explore your relationship with your resistance to pain and sadness.

What I use to numb out is . . .

I tend to numb when . . .

My sadness is . . .

It feels overwhelming when . . .

How I avoid sadness is . . .

How I hide my sadness from others is . . .

The price I've paid for avoiding my own pain/sadness is . . .

The price my partner(s) has paid is . . .

The price my family/friends/kids have paid is . . .

When I'm in emotional pain, it's usually because . . .

What I need most in these moments is . . .

If my pain/sadness had a voice, what it would say to me is . . .

Answering these questions has felt/revealed . . .

What I've been avoiding in my life/relationship/finances/sex life/health is . . .

INTEGRATION EXERCISE

Make a list of all the things you've felt resistance to in the past few days or weeks—certain conversations, activities, or things you've wanted to do (maybe a new habit or routine you've wanted to engage in but have been avoiding).

If you are unsure about what you've felt resistance toward, ask yourself:

What is/are the question(s) I don't want to ask?

What is/are the conversation(s) I don't want to have?

What memories, feelings, experiences have I been avoiding?

Beside each thing you feel resistance to, ask yourself three questions:

What is my resistance trying to protect me from?

What does this protection feel similar to in my past?

Is this an edge I would expand by facing? If so, what action will I take and by when?

THE SOCIAL AGREEMENT OF MALE SILENCE

Who betrayed you, and who have you betrayed? I am always shocked to hear how many men have been physically, verbally, or sexually abused. How many men have seen or witnessed abuse, been forced into abusive dynamics, or grown up in environments where abuse was the norm. What's even more shocking is how many of these men have never told a soul—never had an outlet to work through the pain, anger, or grief of the experience.

When I lead men's weekends, work with clients, or speak with men at conferences, I am inundated with stories of countless men who have lived silently with their pain for years, sometimes even decades. An uncle who took advantage of them as a young boy while camping, a grandfather or coach who would physically or emotionally abuse them, a daycare owner who coerced them into sexual acts with another child, a mother who would slap them and pull their hair whenever they would disobey, a stepbrother who bullied and tormented them, or a father who couldn't control his alcohol-fueled rage.

All these men were ashamed of these betrayals and bought into the agreement that *it's better to hold it in than learn how to heal it out.*

For other men, their silence was not related to abuse. They may have grown up in a household witnessing parents who stayed in a dead marriage, surrounded by slamming doors and passive-aggressive comments, lost a parent to cancer early in life and were never able to grieve, or were forced to act as the mediator and translator between Mom and Dad—all of which can be coded as a betrayal.

Finally, some men are struggling with the weight of their own betrayals. The countless affairs, how they've neglected their wives and children, or the deep shame they've carried for the damage they caused when they themselves were abusive.

Some are afraid of entering into their own grief and sadness for fear of having it consume them or make them weak. There is a narrative adopted by many men which says exploring your past is pointless and working through your pain makes you a pussy.

This couldn't be further from the truth. Men who are able to face their past and heal are able to change course, and are no longer burdened by the deep betrayals they've witnessed or taken part in.

I remember working with a former Navy Seal who was navigating through some of the grief he'd been carrying after seeing his brothers die in battle. He had a decent upbringing, a deep respect for his father, and had come to work with me because his anger and volatility were dominating his relationship—a relationship he wanted to keep but knew he was actively destroying. During one of our sessions, I asked him what happened when someone was killed in battle. How did they grieve the loss of their brother?

"A photo was pinned up on the wall as a reminder for all of us to remain vigilant. Occasionally we'd tell stories, but more often than not, we moved forward," he said.

"No ceremony for him? Nothing?" I asked.

"Nah. Maybe a few moments of silence. We let our actions be the ceremony," he replied.

As we explored how he wanted to grieve his friends, honoring their lives and families, I led him through various exercises in which he was able to reconnect to them and say goodbye on his own terms. To speak out for their lost lives and the vacancy that was left in their place—opening the tap of grief within him that had been glued shut for years. After one such exercise I asked what his experience was and what he learned from it.

He paused and said, “Honestly? I'd rather rush a machine gun nest than do this shit. Grief. Fucking. Sucks.”

We had a good laugh, but in reality, he had summed up the experience of countless men. When it comes to facing the weight of past abuse, divorce, failures, and loss, men have been conditioned to ignore and reject rather than to assimilate and metabolize their internal suffering.

As we explored the anger and grief this man was carrying, he confessed to feeling like he had betrayed the men he stood beside on the battlefield. He couldn't protect them, which carried its own weight, but when they had fallen, he felt as though he had betrayed them again by not truly honoring the lives they had given. He felt a deep and overwhelming sense of responsibility to do something potent with his life after his service—to really make his life count—almost as if the lives of his fallen brothers rested squarely on his shoulders. It left him with a kind of deadness and rage toward himself for his perceived betrayal. He didn't know what to do with it, but he was acting it out on the ones around him.

Through the work, he eventually realized he was verbally and emotionally attacking his partner in an unconscious effort to drive her away. His shadow adopted the story that he was now a man who betrays the people closest to him—better to push the ones he loves away than to see them get hurt.

This is the case for many men. They have betrayed someone they love deeply and carry the bitterness, resentment, and fear of having it happen again. It creates a psycho-emotional storm internally as they fail to understand how or why they could have ever done such a thing.

But when a man is silent about the pain he's experienced from betrayal, he will act it out in some fashion. Much like the man above whose pain and grief were surfacing through his anger and volatility toward the woman he loved, any man who stays silent about his own suffering will inevitably pay the price—or offload that price onto the world around him.

Break the silence of your own suffering and betrayals respectfully, diligently, and in a manner that forces you to meet your edge. Fully acknowledge the impact of the betrayals you've experienced, without letting them become the cornerstone of your identity. Surround yourself with men who will speak the truth about their suffering and are willing to engage in productive dialogue about how they learned to carry their pain more effectively—*to work with the pain, rather than having it work you.* Be with men who will not only see and hear your pain, but will also confront and challenge you to grieve when needed while calling you out of the emotional basement if you've let self-pity and resentment take the lead. Let go of trying to save the men and women around you who are clearly suffering but unwilling to face it.

The aim here is not to air your dirty laundry or to constantly navel gaze at your past, but rather to decisively and concretely commit to moving your suffering and pain from the realm of the shadow, from the hidden and unspoken recesses of your life, into the light of consciousness, where it can be understood, owned, and integrated.

INTEGRATION EXERCISE

Make a list of what you've been silent about in your life, past and present. What have you avoided sharing, being honest about, and revealing to others? Now, pick a trusted person in your life and share one of the things you've kept quiet about, being honest about the impact it had on you. Try sharing one new thing with someone each week, or even one each day for a month.

BECOME A TRAUMA-INFORMED MAN

Learn how to regulate your nervous system, or your nervous system will regulate your life (likely not in the way you want).

For a number of years I travelled across North America hosting live events, seminars, and transformational workshops. At some point in the event or workshop I would ask all the men to raise their hand if they were dating, or had dated, someone who had experienced some form of trauma. On average about 80 percent of the men would raise their hands. We would talk about their experience in the relationship, the impact trauma or adverse events had had on the people they dated, and what it was like for them to be on the other side of a partner's behavior that was sometimes erratic and hard to understand. They told stories of partners who had experienced sexual abuse, physical violence, or an abusive past partner. Many of the men would talk about being unsure as to how they could be of service and were often angry about the experiences their loved ones had endured.

After the men described some of the events their partners had experienced and some of the residual impacts and behaviors they were left with, I would ask the men to reflect on their own lives—had they experienced similar events? Had they as men experienced adverse events growing up that had shaped the way they behaved at work, in relationships, and in social environments? Again, I would ask the men to raise their hand if they had experienced some form of bullying, abandonment, or abuse (verbal, physical, or sexual) in their life, and without fail the number of hands that went up in the room was about the same.

Many of these men had come to the workshop in search of change. Men wanting to lead from their masculine core, men in search of purpose and more quality relationships, and men in search of an answer to the question, "Why can't I get my life together?" Many of these men felt disempowered and frustrated and were looking for a reason that would explain why they had been struggling for so long. They wanted to better themselves as men and were ready to do the work, but they felt largely incapable of describing why their life didn't look the way they wanted it to.

For some men, the answer was that they hadn't put the work in. They knew the path they needed to take but hadn't yet found the motivation to hit the accelerator and move forward. For others there was a mass of confusion. There were some wildly successful men who had built empires but were actively sabotaging everything they'd spent years developing, and other men who had never been able to get things off the ground.

There was a strange phenomenon I would encounter workshop after workshop, man after man. These men were trying to figure out why their lives were in disarray, trying to figure out why they continued to sabotage relationship after relationship, business after business, but they had never considered that the trauma they experienced in childhood could possibly have an impact on their lives in the present moment.

One man at a workshop in Toronto, Canada, described how he was miserable in his marriage. He was in his early fifties, had been with his second wife for several years, but had been living in the basement for the past two years because they couldn't seem to get along. He had two kids from the previous marriage: one was in college, and the other, in high school, lived with him. When I inquired about his upbringing and what his parents were like, he replied, "I had a pretty normal childhood. My parents were fine"—the standard answer for a man who saw little value in inspecting his youth.

"What was their marriage like?" I inquired. "What kind of challenges did they face as a couple?" I pressed to see if he was open to talking about it.

"I dunno, I guess the normal stuff. My dad worked a lot and had a pretty bad temper. My mom stayed at home, didn't work and raised the kids. They got along for the most part."

"And what about when they didn't get along?" I asked.

"Well, when they didn't get along, I guess it wasn't great. Like I said, my old man had a pretty bad temper, so when they didn't get along, he could be an asshole," he said while he laughed, almost as if his father being an asshole was funny, but clearly because he was uncomfortable admitting the truth.

"Okay," I said, "why don't you tell the men in this room what kind of asshole your father was."

Now, there are moments in every man's life when he is pressed face to face with the demons of his past. Moments when he has to decide as a man whether he is going to enter in the dark lair of what his younger self promised he would never talk about, face, or think about again. Moments when a man is pushed into a confrontation with everything he prayed he could let go of or leave unseen. This was one of those moments, and all the men in the room could feel it. Was he going to hide from the truth of his past, or could he stand and face it?

"Really? Do I have to?" he asked, trying to downplay the discomfort he was clearly experiencing.

"Only if you want to, but definitely if it's what you least want to do," I replied.

The man paused, contemplating whether he was going to dive into the deep end, and after a few moments, he said:

"He was . . . well, he was the kind of asshole who would yell at my mom. When he thought she had done something wrong he would start in on her, criticizing her, getting louder and louder, backing her into a corner or against the kitchen counter. He was always pointing his fucking finger at her, poking it into her face and chest, threatening her but never really getting physically violent with her." His face was now flushed with rage and embarrassment.

"And what about you?" I asked. "What kind of asshole was he to you?"

"To me? I don't want to talk about that. It's not important," he said, glaring at me as if to say, *Don't you fucking dare.*

"Okay. As I said, only if you want to. I *am* curious about why it's not important though."

He paused.

Finally, he said, "Because I don't want to let him take up any more time in my life. He's dead, I moved on, his actions were on him to live with, not me."

And there it was, the belief that so many cling to—*If I deny that my abuser's actions had any impact on me, then they don't have any power over me.*

This man decided to walk into the fire, proceeded to talk about his father's actions, and sat stoically in the middle of the room as 150 men listened to his story. His father had physically abused him as a child, locked him outside without a jacket or gloves in the freezing Canadian winter when he was out of line, duct taped him to chairs when he was too rambunctious, and verbally eviscerated him for poor grades, sports performances, and anything else his father deemed to be substandard.

At some point, the boy who was abused decided that the only way to deal with the trauma and pain his father dished out to him was to pretend it didn't affect him. He became hard, closed off, and immune to people's disappointment and frustration, and he pushed away any bid for emotional closeness. This had spilled into his marriage, where he was cold and disconnected. Although he desperately wanted to be close to his wife, he found himself interpreting her words and actions as attacks and insults—something he dealt with by walling himself off.

But here was the catch: He had convinced himself that his childhood had nothing to do with his failed marriages. Nothing to do with his unwillingness to hear his wife's desperate pleas for compassion, nothing to do with his complete disregard for her feelings (or his own), and nothing to do with why he was fifty years old and had essentially cut himself off from anyone who got too close to him.

He dealt with his trauma the way countless men do—by becoming a master of pretending like it never happened or couldn't possibly have had an impact.

After his story, and the stories of a few other men who had been through hell, we defined trauma—*a deeply distressing or disturbing experience*—and explored how trauma disrupts the body's natural ability to regulate itself and determine whether any given environment or circumstance is ultimately safe.

It's helpful to know that there are three types of trauma: *acute, chronic,* and *complex.*

Acute trauma refers to a single, traumatic incident that happens in your life that has a clear beginning, middle, and end. Acute trauma can affect people in a number of ways: some people have immediate symptoms that require professional support and intervention, while others don't have much of a trauma response at all. Some people develop symptoms several weeks or months after the event.

Acute traumas may include events like:

- Car accident
- Sexual assault or rape
- Physical altercation
- Serious injury
- Natural disaster
- Witnessing a violent event

Chronic trauma is a result of witnessing or being part of a repeated or prolonged distressing event. This may be reoccurring sexual abuse, bullying, domestic violence, serious health issues, or exposure to extreme situations, such as a war. The symptoms of chronic trauma often appear after a long time, sometimes even years after the event, and can include extreme anger, flashbacks, body aches, headaches, outbursts, anxiety, and high levels of fatigue. Symptoms are often accompanied by trust issues, which can make it more challenging for the individual to maintain healthy relationships or even employment.

Complex trauma is a result of exposure to varied and multiple traumatic events or experiences. It can be seen in people who have experienced child abuse, neglect, domestic violence, and other repetitive situations, impacting the individual's overall health and performance.

In lay terms: *trauma creates isolation and despair, often with the belief that there is no hope of recovery from the trauma we experienced.*

The reality of trauma is that it can alter your nervous system's perception of safety. This means you don't have to *think* you are scared, unsafe, or under attack for your body to react with fear or panic as if you really *are* unsafe or under attack.

This happens because your nervous system is constantly taking in sensory information from your external and internal environments, using this information to gauge your level of safety and the level of risk you are experiencing. Dr. Stephen Porges, professor of psychiatry and author of *The Polyvagal Theory*, developed a concept called *neuroception*, which describes how your brain and the neural circuits within determine whether any given situation is dangerous, safe, or potentially life threatening.

According to Dr. Porges, "Even though you may not be aware of danger on a cognitive level, on a neurophysiological level your body has already started a sequence of neural processes that can lead to fight/flight/freeze." When we experience trauma, it can cause a disruption to our neuroception and our ability to properly discern whether simple things like a conversation, coffee shop, or social gathering are safe or dangerous. We can begin to take small conflicts with our loved ones out of context, and our body can respond to these situations as if we are in a life-and-death situation. Trauma can create faulty interpretation of the information received through our neuroceptive system. Simply put, it distorts the information you're receiving externally and internally, altering your ability to know for sure whether you are safe, secure, and grounded.

A trauma-informed man is one who understands the impact and ramifications that past experiences can have on present-day decisions and responses—both within himself and the people around him. Do not pretend that the past has nothing to do with your present; admit that they may be entangled and aim to reconcile with the past you've been avoiding.

One of the best things you can do for yourself, regardless of whether you've experienced trauma, is to learn how to regulate your nervous system. To do this will require you to develop a base understanding of when and how you move into a fight/flight/freeze response and be able to prioritize practices to restore balance within your system.

Know that for a period your body and brain may be moving in different directions. If you have not worked to develop the skill of regulating your mind and body, you may think one thing but find yourself doing the opposite. You may cognitively know the relationship you're in is outstanding while your body is continuously pulling you away, trying to protect you from unseen and hidden threat. Be willing to engage in conversations with a trusted therapist or mentor who knows how to traverse the territory of trauma and can give you real tools and practices to regulate your nervous system and mind. Set yourself to the task of learning how to regulate your body and implement daily practices that will bring your nervous system into balance.

Lastly, find someone to work with. Not because you are broken, damaged, or defective—you're not, I assure you. But you do have parts of your body, psyche, and heart that are carrying such deep pain or sorrow that it can feel like you're beyond repair. I get it, I've been there. I had to realize I wasn't a broken man, just a man who had been wounded and never patched up. Find someone to work with so you can learn the tools to navigate the unique and specific impact that trauma can have on your mind, body, thoughts, decisions, and communication. Make sure you do your diligence in finding someone who helps you get results. The same is true in business and therapy: results matter.

In the words of one of the greatest gestalt practitioners I know, Duey Freeman: *Our bodies will express trauma either consciously or subconsciously.* This truly is not a choice; we will express it regardless of whether we want to or not. A trauma-informed man chooses to dig deep enough internally and externally to work through his trauma so his trauma isn't working his life.

INTEGRATION EXERCISE

Practice regulation. Whether you have experienced trauma or not, learning how to regulate your nervous system is an absolutely vital skill. It will allow you to better cope with stress and know when you've reached a limit and need to re-orient yourself before continuing a conversation or interaction. The aim here is to develop resiliency and a kind of anti-fragile nature so you can better lead yourself and those around you.

Step one: Learn the cues. When you experience repeated or extended periods of stress, you can experience nervous system dysregulation. This term refers to the nervous system's inability to bring itself back to a normal, regulated state after stress.

The signs of dysregulation include physical activation like muscle tension, chronic fatigue, exhaustion, clenched jaw, insomnia, migraines, and being overly sensitive to loud sounds or bright lights.

When your nervous system is dysregulated, you might find yourself more prone to intense shame, fear, panic, mood swings, overwhelm, anxiety, aggression, and confusion. It's not uncommon for people to feel numb, spaced out, disconnected, and to have a heightened desire to isolate entirely or else become overly needy.

Step two: Restore balance. Reground yourself in the moment using the breath. Sit on the floor or plant your feet firmly on the ground (in the grass, water, sand, or on the floor) and use the box breath (inhale for a count of four, hold at the top of the inhale for a count of four, exhale for a count of four, hold for four: 4-4-4-4).

Another breathing exercise that has been shown to ground and restore balance in the nervous system is to exhale for longer than you inhale, like this: inhale (through the nose) for a count of four, hold for a count of two, exhale (lightly through the mouth) for a count of six, hold for a count of two.

Step three: Practice daily. Pick an active practice like breathwork, meditation, or cold showers, and connect to your nervous system's response while you do the activity.

SHAME: FUEL FOR SABOTAGE

Sean is describing a fight he had with his wife a few days before our session. He forgot to enroll his son into the class field trip, and his wife asked him why he hadn't followed through with it after she reminded him a few days before the deadline. Sean immediately got angry with his wife, becoming defensive and verbally jabbing back, saying that he only forgot because he was picking up for her slack around the house. Sean knew he was over-the-top angry but couldn't figure out why he became so aggressive with her. She disengaged from the argument, which pissed him off even more. He continued to escalate by telling his wife she wasn't "allowed" to just pick a fight and walk away. He began to ridicule his wife for how she had been behaving lately and found himself listing all the small grievances he had with her. Sean could feel himself physically becoming hotter and was observing his volatility almost as if he was a passenger in the vehicle of his own mind and body. He knew he was in the wrong, knew he was out of control, but couldn't seem to stop.

What Sean couldn't see was that he wasn't angry at her—he was ashamed of himself.

Sean was criticized and put down frequently as a boy. Growing up he felt like he could never get things right and had become hypercritical of himself. So, when his wife pointed out that he had missed something, asking him what had happened, Sean felt ashamed not because he had made a mistake, but because on some level he felt like he *was* the mistake.

Sean was largely unaware that he was bypassing his shame and quickly moving into defensive anger followed by hostile aggression—a strategy he unconsciously developed to protect himself from the criticism he received growing up.

When I asked Sean when he felt ashamed and what triggered his shame, he was unable to answer. When I asked him what shame felt like for him, he stared blankly and responded, "I really have no idea. I know when I'm angry, happy, and sad . . . but I really don't know what shame even feels like."

This is the case for many of us. When we feel shame, we have an instinctual reaction to get away from it as quickly as possible—leaving many of us in the dark, completely unaware of when we are acting and responding from shame. This is true for many men because we equate who we are with what we do. So, when we do something wrong, we believe that it's not our action that's wrong, but us. As John Bradshaw, author of *Healing the Shame That Binds Us*, said: "Guilt says I've done something wrong; shame says there is something wrong with me. Guilt says I've made a mistake; shame says I am a mistake. Guilt says what I did was not good; shame says I am no good."

Shame can act like alcohol for your emotions, numbing you out to its presence, pushing down the truth of how you are feeling. It can act as an emotional suppressant and blind you from being able to see the emotion behind the shame. When we ignore shame for long enough, letting it fester and build, it will eventually consume us.

However, not all shame is bad. Some shame shows up to engage our remorse, aiding us in correcting our behavior. Shame and guilt act as the bumpers of life, ensuring we are living moral and honorable lives. The aim is not to eradicate your shame but rather to build a deep awareness of it, so you know when it's pulling the strings of your actions.

In simple terms, how you deal with your shame is by acknowledging its existence. Do not bury the shame you feel, but also don't let it grow to the point of consuming you. You may have done something wrong, but *you* are not wrong. Get to know and confront the distortions that shame creates within.

Here are a few examples of shame-based mental distortions.

Hypervigilant need to be right. You can't make a mistake, or else. Because of this, you are constantly needing to reaffirm your point and prove that you're right.

Either/or thinking. Most things are perceived as extremes. There is rarely any middle ground, and you are not exempt from this extreme judgment. You're either good or bad, absolutely crushing it or a complete disaster. There is no room for error, and things are seen as black and white. Nuance is destroyed.

Catastrophic thinking. Small mistakes are world ending. Your wife wanting to talk means she wants a divorce, and "what ifs" are a constant thought.

Taking it personally. Most things get personalized, and you're constantly comparing yourself to others because you don't want to self-reference. When your partner is upset, it must be your fault, or your problem to fix.

Shoulda, woulda, coulda. You are constantly reflecting on what you should have done, could have done better, or would have done if only.

Create space between who you are and what you've done. Just because you did something wrong doesn't mean you are wrong. Look at your actions objectively and own the mistakes you may have made. Say you lied to your partner about why you came home late from work and feel ashamed for not telling the truth. You can learn from your mistake and honor that you're ashamed of your actions by taking ownership and saying something like, "I lied about why I got home late from work last night" instead of, "I am a lying piece of crap and always fuck up." The first allows you to acknowledge your mistake, identifying why you feel ashamed and creating space to apologize, while the second leaves little to no room for forgiveness as you are fully in the seat of the victim. This will likely require you to share your shame, something most people find to be an incredible challenge.

When you separate your actions from who you are as a man, you can see the truth of why you made the mistakes in the first place. You'll be able to see that you didn't lie to your partner because you're the worst human being on the planet; you lied because you were self-sabotaging on some level. Maybe things had been going really well lately and you're not used to the kind of stability you have in the relationship, so you threw a wrench in the mix. Maybe you lost track of time working on a project for the third day in a row and didn't want her to be disappointed or upset with you, so you made something up to avoid "getting into trouble." Regardless of the reason, understanding and accepting why you did it allows you to learn the lesson so you can do better next time.

Lastly, execute all of this with empathy. You may want to be perfect, but perfection is almost always tied to punishment. A man who is obsessed with being perfect is often a man looking for a reason to punish himself. Let go of the punishment and embrace the empathy of being a man dedicated to betterment.

INTEGRATION EXERCISE

Reprogramming shameful thought patterns is essential.

1) Think about something you normally shame yourself for (being overweight, not good enough sexually, being a failure as a father or partner . . .).

2) Confront and interrupt. Thoughts can be interrupted and confronted, much like the annoying guy at the bar. When the thought arises, interrupt it by saying *enough* either mentally in your mind or verbally out loud. This should be forceful, yet kind. You are not threatening or being aggressive, simply setting a firm and clear boundary. ENOUGH. Repeat it a few times.

3) Replace the thought. Reframe the thought or replace the thought with what you want to think instead. "You are working on it." Or, "It's okay to fail, and okay to be imperfect." Or, "This is annoying, and it will be overcome." You will need to find your own reframe based on the shameful thoughts you have. Find your own language, make the thoughts positive, and remember to confront the shameful thought first.

THE GOLD IN THE SHADOW

There is no growth, no gold, and no change without confrontation: confronting your fears, confronting the fact that you haven't forgiven yourself or another for a betrayal, confronting the grief you've let fester unattended within, and confronting the decisions, actions, and conversations you've desperately tried to avoid.

As I've discovered over the years: *no confrontation = no actualizing of potential.*

Confrontation is the threshold of potential. It is the price we must be willing to pay in order to pass through the gates of exploring the uncharted territory of our capacities, fears, and limitations. We must know with the fullest of our mind, heart, and soul that confrontation is a necessary task. In fact, it might be *the* task. We must confront our inferiorities because these are the aspects we've deemed to be lower in rank or quality. They are the parts of our body, mind, and personality that we consistently try to hide or compensate for, but also the place where the psychological gold resides.

But taking aim at rectifying and addressing your inferiorities is no small piece of work. Think about what makes you feel small, weak, and less than others. What aspects of your identity do you vehemently dislike? What have you done to get rid of that feeling or belief? Maybe you find yourself avoiding certain people at work or holding onto disappointment and resentment toward your partner—all because you won't engage in a conversation you know you need to have but are afraid of the possible confrontation.

Confronting one's own lethargy or self-critical nature might be the primal tussle you are being asked to engage in, to break loose some of the self-reliance lying dormant in your shadow. Maybe you need to confront your fear of rejection, embarrassment, or the unmet and unprocessed shame you've harbored for decades about your sexual desires. I've worked with countless men who have spent years and decades of their life "in the closet," hiding the truth about their own sexuality and sexual desires. The thought of confronting the truth about being gay or bisexual, having to tell their family or reveal something they have known for years to their wife, seems like an overwhelming and seemingly impossible task. Regardless of the confrontation, it can be done, and must be done, in order to step into a more complete, whole version of yourself as a man.

Potential, regardless of where you believe it to reside, demands that you go toe to toe with the beast of fear. You must first identify what specifically you are afraid of, why you're afraid of it, and consciously choose to engage with that fear. Without this, you will be lost in the haze of confusion—unsure of where to start, what action to take, or why you should even pursue this evolution at all. When you confront your fears and face your insecurities, you prove to yourself that you are capable of something you thought impossible—the act of bringing potential into being. To think, act, behave, respond, or lead in a way you previously didn't believe was possible for you.

Start by taking stock of your perceived inferiorities and what you fear most. List out the qualities, behaviors, and traits you have ranked lowest. Do you see your intelligence as something that is inferior? Do you think you lack assertiveness or the ability to be direct?

If you are unsure about this, inquire with the people you trust most in your life. Ask a close male friend to be as direct as possible and solicit his perspective about what aspect of your personality and your life you need to confront. Ask them, "What fear/truth/decision or insecurity do you think I need to confront?" Or, "What do you think I've been avoiding that I need to confront?"

If you are someone who lacks assertiveness and is afraid of rejection, spend a week or month committing to rejection therapy—making daily asks of your team members, spouse, friends, family, and community. This way you confront your fear of being told "no" and can build up tolerance and resilience in the face of what you least wish to confront. If you have avoided physical strength and see your body as being inferior, commit to thirty days of burpees or jump squats, forcing yourself to confront the belief of being weak. Maybe what you've been afraid to confront is embarking on the journey of forgiving your father for his behavior when you were a child, or finding forgiveness for yourself or your partner after an affair.

Finally, notice how resistant you become at the thought of this confrontation. There will be an immediate desire to back down or conveniently forget about the commitment. On the other hand, some men will be excited for the confrontation, thinking it will involve force or aggression, only to realize their confrontation is entirely about learning to surrender, be more compassionate, or allow others to contribute. Sometimes we view letting go as a weakness, as inferiority itself, and so it is the very thing we must confront. If you've ever loved someone who was an addict, letting go is one of the most difficult yet necessary things you are faced with.

When this confrontation manifests, be it through the circumstances of your life or your own choosing, do not waste it. Here you are presented with the opportunity to reveal a more competent, potent, and fully actualized version of yourself. Remember—wholeness happens because of confrontation, not because of its absence.

INTEGRATION EXERCISE

1) Make a list of the aspects, traits, or beliefs that you think are inferior about yourself. Do you lack confidence? Assertiveness? The willingness to allow or go with the flow? Maybe you view your body or physical strength as being inferior?

    The fear I haven't been willing to face is . . .

    If I was being brutally honest, I feel inferior when . . .

    I am insecure about . . .

    What I know I could do to confront that insecurity is . . .

    The action I will take is . . .

2) Ask a close friend or family member, "What fear or insecurity do you think I need to confront?"

3) Write out a confrontation commitment, no more than a couple of sentences, and read the commitment out loud each morning. "Today, I commit to confronting . . ."

MOVE FROM MEDICATE TO MEDITATE

We are the children of medicated men and have adopted a medicated way of living. If you're like some men, you use booze to socialize, weed to relax, sugar to feel satiated, porn to release pent-up sexual frustration or stress, and any number of pharmaceuticals to regulate your mind and body. The endless options for TV series and movies occupy real estate in your daily life, while social media has quickly hijacked your morning and evening routines—giving you a false sense of connection as you scroll through other people's lives while silently sitting next to someone you'd say is important to you, but who you often feel the furthest from. As boredom, monotonous routines, and petty frustrations mount, something must be done to alleviate the all-too-familiar feelings of despair, rage, and loneliness that we have become immersed in because of our overconsumption of other people's online commentary.

These coping mechanisms are tools to help numb out the banal and overly domesticated life most have been sold and told to inhabit. If left unattended to, these mechanisms become necessary for finding reprieve from the unique kind of hell we create when living inside the bars of this domesticated prison. Tools we use to regulate our overtaxed, overworked, stressed-out, disengaged, and under-rested nervous system—often more nervous than a functional system.

The truth is that a man who is overly reliant on coping mechanisms is a diminished man. He is easier to control and less likely to speak out about the circumstances he finds unsavory in his life and the society he inhabits. Simply put, a medicated man is less of a threat to the norms of modern-day society. A medicated man is less likely to speak up against injustice, less likely to oppose tyranny, and less likely to be effective enough to lead his own family.

You've probably felt this at some point in your life, maybe even recently. You find yourself feeling low on energy, mildly depressed or anxious, angry or bored, and automatically turn to something to alleviate your problem. You get overwhelmed due to a situation at work, the moron in the checkout line at the grocery store, or a challenge in your relationship and immediately grab a beer, light a joint, or turn on whatever TV show currently has your attention.

As an example, notice what you turn to when you and your partner have an argument. What's the first thing you want? Do you immediately pick up your phone and doomscroll through social media, falling into a few thirst traps on Instagram or Snapchat—fantasizing about how much easier or better life would be if only you were the one with the bikini-clad woman sporting the inspirational quotes in her caption? Do you walk into the kitchen and crack a beer? Turn on the TV and tune out the pain? Nowadays there are more metaphorical pills than problems.

But the medication isn't the problem. The real problem is that most men have forgotten how to live a meditative life. A life rich with the inherent medicine and nourishment of intimacy, connection, nature, adventure, building things that matter, along with the generative habits and rituals essential to refuel their system. Instead, we have outsourced our capacity to regulate our mind, body, and nervous system and are immersed in a culture where individuals and corporations alike are quick to capitalize on our zombie-like reaction to anything undesirable.

We as men have become castrated, ineffective, and highly domesticated at the hands of a society willing to bankroll and profit from our cornucopia of coping mechanisms.

Ultimately there are two ways to deal with your problems and regulate your internal system: unconsciously through coping mechanisms or consciously with generative habits.

The task you are faced with is learning how to transmute your coping mechanisms into more strengthening and sustaining rituals. Say you have a habit of eating late at night or watching porn before bed as a means of scrubbing away the drudgery of the day. This coping mechanism, over time and through very real and sustained effort, can be replaced by a meditation practice, breathwork, cold shower, infrared sauna, tai chi, or any number of other rituals that will be more conducive to regulating your mind and body—ultimately putting you, rather than some external tool, at the helm of creating inner peace.

The aim here is not to change all habits all at once.

To begin, intentionally choose a coping mechanism that feels conquerable, leaving the more engrained coping mechanisms for when you've built some momentum and resiliency. For example, I used to wake up and immediately check my email, which almost always led to spending the first thirty to forty-five minutes of my day on social media. This was a coping mechanism for the anxiousness I often felt in the morning as I woke up thinking about everything I needed to do for work. I committed to spending at least one month getting up and doing thirty minutes of breathwork and yoga in the morning instead. To be honest, it was daunting the first few weeks. It was challenging to sit and breathe while my brain and body kicked and screamed about the change, eager to get on social media or check my email, pleading for the slow drip of dopamine these platforms have conditioned us with.

Thankfully over time it got easier. I found myself waking up and craving the silence, peace, and ritualistic morning breathing. I felt more at ease, in control, and energized to tackle my task list, and I even found that I needed less coffee to do so. Over the years I have given up drinking alcohol entirely, ended my addiction to porn, stopped smoking weed, and significantly reduced how much TV and social media I consume. In their place I have taken up boxing, yoga, breathwork, meditation, tai chi, playing an instrument, and various other rituals to help sustain my well-being. My family, business, marriage, and child all benefit because of these changes. It in no way makes me a perfect man, but it certainly makes me a more effective and valuable man—something that has also brought with it a deep level of fulfillment and joy that was lacking before.

INTEGRATION EXERCISE

Consciously and intentionally shift your medicating habits to more meditation-oriented rituals. This week, choose one medicating habit and replace it with a more expansive or generative ritual. Turn off your phone for an entire day, delete social media for a week, commit to not watching porn or drinking for a week, and replace it with something that will reconnect you to your body, mission, and purpose—journaling, meditation, breathwork, yoga, working out, or some other restorative practice. Bonus points for enlisting another man in this exercise and creating some accountability.

PART 2

LEADING IN SEX, WOMEN & INTIMACY

CHAPTER 5

SHADOW OF THE MOTHER

"A mother is the truest friend we have, when trials heavy and sudden fall upon us; when adversity takes the place of prosperity; when friends desert us; when trouble thickens around us, still will she cling to us, and endeavor by her kind precepts and counsels to dissipate the clouds of darkness, and cause peace to return to our hearts."

WASHINGTON IRVING

LYLE WAS SEATED on the floor in the middle of the room, surrounded by a circle of thirty men attending a men's weekend I was running in British Columbia. He was engaged to be married within the next year but had a history of paying for prostitutes and virtual cam girls and had been caught by his fiancé. Lyle had come to the weekend trying to figure out why he kept going back to these women.

As I worked with Lyle, I could see how many of the men related to parts of his story. He had historically chased women he thought were "out of his league," becoming needy and pedestalling them, or would find himself in relationships with women he was half interested in. When he met his fiancé, he committed to stop spending money on virtual sex but found the habit harder to kick than expected. He was incredibly harsh on himself, lacked clarity about what he wanted, and had been relatively successful in his career, but he still felt deeply miserable.

"Everything looks pretty great in my life, but I'm still not happy," he said at one point, to which some of the men nodded as if to say, "Same here."

I asked him to describe what he would do with the women he hired.

"Well, most of the time I get some drugs, a hotel room, and just . . . spend time with them. We talk, occasionally I'll have sex with them, but most of the time it just feels good to hang out with them, talk about our lives, and relax. It's embarrassing to say, but sometimes I just want to put my head in their lap or have them hold me while we talk. There's something comforting about it."

Lyle had grown up with a very strict mother who demanded high performance from him. As a boy, she would get him up at 5:30 a.m., make him practice violin (which he didn't even enjoy), work on a second language (French), then prep his own lunch, all before heading out to school. This started when he was six or seven years old, only a few years after his parents (who were his adopted parents) had divorced. When Lyle was a boy and would get emotional or wanted attention, his mother—who was loving to a degree—would tell him not to feel what he was feeling. "Don't be sad" and "You shouldn't be angry" were reoccurring themes he would hear.

Lyle had developed a deep anger and distrust toward his adopted mother. "Her emotions were all over the place," he said as I worked with him in front of the group. "She was always afraid, anxious, worrying, and stressed out. She had a lot of sadness and it felt like I always had to take care of her."

As we dug deeper into his childhood, Lyle disclosed that he was put up for adoption by his birth mother the day he was born.

"What do you know about your birth?" I asked.

"Apparently, I was put up for adoption but there wasn't anyone available yet. From what I know, I was held at the hospital for over a month while they looked for someone to adopt me and then taken care of for another few months by child services until they found someone."

"So, the first few months of your life were pretty lonely, hey?" I said.

"Well, yeah. I guess I hadn't thought about it that way," he replied.

As we continued to explore, I walked Lyle through an exercise imagining himself as a man walking back into the hospital where he was born, seeing himself as a baby swaddled up in a blanket, and asked him to connect to that newborn child.

"What do you see?" I asked.

"He's just alone," Lyle responded. "Like, entirely alone. It's devastating. How could anyone do that to a kid? Just leave them alone like that." Tears were now streaming down his face.

"What would you say to that boy?" I asked. "If you were standing in that room and that was your son, what would you do?"

"I'd just hold him," Lyle replied. "He just needs to be held. He shouldn't be alone. I'd hold him and tell him that he's loved and not alone." Lyle broke down as the men around him were still, honoring the hidden pain he had been carrying.

Here was a man who had not only been shut down emotionally by the woman who adopted him, but who was abandoned by the woman who brought him into the world. As a result he had developed a deep wound of betrayal and felt unsafe with women.

He had an unconscious mistrust of women—craving them and seeking their affection while simultaneously believing that he would be betrayed or abandoned. And so, he paid for closeness because it felt much safer than building it in his relationship.

Lyle, like many men, never experienced the strong bond he needed to build trust and respect for the feminine. In his shadow were all the qualities of a woman or mother that he never received—traits like compassion, nurturing, understanding, and kindness—along with a deep fear and sadness. As a result, Lyle never developed these aspects in his own psyche—they were hidden from him, directing his actions and behaviors when he interacted with women. He was internally harsh with himself, constantly shaming himself whenever he screwed up and constantly picking himself apart when things weren't perfect. He was afraid to ask his fiancé for what he needed and had built up resentment toward her and the relationship for not fulfilling something he hadn't directly expressed or known how to create. When disconnection or conflict happened with his fiancé, it was in these moments—the moments when he felt anxiety and anger toward her, blaming her for his loneliness—that he would turn to the comfort and safety of paying for a woman's attention, fantasize about being close to a woman, or seek out a woman's company online.

Now, your story is probably very different from Lyle's, but perhaps there are some similarities. Maybe your mother was a wonderful woman who was very encouraging but passed away when you were a teenager, leaving you afraid to lose the women you love. Perhaps your mother was emotionally controlling, incessantly critical, overly emotional, or put you in the position of having to take care of her. Or maybe she was distant and unemotional, rarely giving you love or physical affection. Perhaps she put you on such a high pedestal that you could do no wrong, or was so consumed by the drama of her own life that you barely knew her. Regardless of the circumstances, your mother will have directly impacted the way you view, treat, and interact with women.

THE MOTHER AND THE ANIMA

Jung believed that resting inside of our mind are the opposing sexual capacities known as the anima and animus, or the feminine and masculine, respectively. The anima represents the unconscious side of a man's mind and comprises the feminine qualities or image of the feminine within a man's psyche and mind, embodying everything he doesn't know about himself. The anima, according to Jung, is "the personification of all feminine psychological tendencies in a man's psyche, such as the value of feelings and moods, prophetic hunches, receptiveness to the irrational, capacity for personal life, feeling for nature and, last but not least, his relation toward the unconscious." As a rule, the anima within a man is shaped by his mother.

The anima, in its positive form, is responsible for helping a man find the right partner, pull out hidden facts about himself from the psyche, enrich his life with beauty and vitality, cultivate a deep connection to nature, and exercise compassion and spontaneity—all valuable traits and qualities. In its negative form, it can cause a man to be highly volatile, irrational, confused about what he wants, and lacking in self-compassion or joy, while leaving him susceptible to his moods and emotions. He can be brooding—joyful one moment and shut down the next—or find himself caught in the net of complete and utter hopelessness.

In our modern culture there are conflicting narratives that constantly aim to constrict men into either being all animus (masculine) or significantly more anima (feminine). Much of the mainstream rhetoric now conspires to make men more feminine. Social media, dating advice, and most mainstream sources look at the problems within male culture and tell men that the solution is to be more vulnerable, overly empathetic to others, and to disconnect from their innate ability to be assertive. Not truly understanding the issue, mainstream culture advocates for men to disconnect from and degrade their own masculine essence and core. But the problem isn't that men need to be less masculine and more feminine—the problem is that men haven't been taught how to be masculine in the first place, or how to honor the feminine within themselves. This tends to build passive, emotional men who avoid their masculine qualities, allowing their anima to be all-consuming and forward facing.

The aim here is neither to reject the feminine qualities of life nor to adopt them to such a degree that you castrate your own masculine essence.

The aim is to bring balance and order to the chaos within yourself.

To do this, you must be willing to look at how your primary relationship to the feminine was forged—through your mother (or the person who played the maternal role in your life). Your mother acted as the blueprint for developing your relationship to women and the feminine both externally and internally. The aim here is not to blame her for your problems or to complain about her parenting. This will get you nowhere. Even if she was perfect in your eyes, the aim is to understand the feminine by understanding the person who modeled it and created the first psychological imprint in your formative years.

The role of the archetypal mother is to be nurturing, caretaking, and a place of reprieve from the chaos of the world. She is the embodiment of life and birth, and a container where a boy learns (consciously and unconsciously) what to expect from women. Most importantly, a mother will directly influence the development of your nervous system and the development of your unconscious mind.

As Jung said in *Man and His Symbols*, a man who had bad experiences with his mother—maybe she was neglectful, volatile, critical, or unpredictable—will be more prone to irritability, uncertainty, depressed moods, insecurity, and overly sensitive or touchy. Often at the core of this man's dysfunction is a hopeless kind of confusion, as if nothing makes any sense or matters, and his inner dialogue can be harsh and demeaning. If he is able to confront and overcome the assaults within himself, it can aid in reinforcing his masculinity. These men often have a very cold, calculated, and factual view of life, lacking the depth of warmth and feeling in the psyche.

A man who had a good experience with his mother, maybe too good, can become very effeminate in nature, be preyed upon or taken advantage of by women, and will usually struggle to cope with or want to face the hardships of life. These men are prone to reflecting and thinking about life so much that they struggle to live it fully.

Without shame or self-criticism, reflect for a moment on the statements above and take note of what sounds familiar from your own behavior. If you're honest, are you often moody and emotionally volatile? Are you shut off, cold, and overly calculating? Or do you find yourself often defaulting to viewing life as hopeless, overwhelming, and deeply confusing? This information will be useful as you read on.

UNDERSTANDING MOM'S IMPRINT

Chase was married and had a newborn son. For the past year Chase had been experiencing a lot of emotional volatility. He had fits of rage, moodiness, and reactivity, which was not only out of character for him but had become much more prominent with the arrival of his boy. He had a short temper with his wife, found himself isolating from his friends, and had become even more hostile toward himself, describing his inner dialogue as a war zone. He grew up in a traditional Jewish household until his parents divorced when he was twelve.

As we explored his upbringing, something he was initially resistant to do, Chase talked about his father's absence and the pressure his mother put on him to help around the home. At first the only thing he would say about his mother was that he "loved her very much, even though she could be infuriating at times." He described their relationship as being close, but burdensome. Even as a forty-one-year-old man, his mother expected him to call her multiple times per week. She had never remarried and told him it was his job as the oldest son to take care of her—something he'd been doing since he was a boy. As he said in one session, "There's nothing like the guilt of a Jewish mother." He meant it in an endearing manner, but clearly he had been worn thin from the guilt and shame she had soaked his psyche in for decades.

As we dug in further, Chase admitted that his mother was very demanding of him; she needed a lot of his attention, and sometimes he found it impossible to be around her. When his father left, his mother enlisted twelve-year-old Chase as the new head of the household, making him rub her shoulders on the weekend, pay the bills, and dish out discipline and punishment to his younger siblings—something they had come to resent him for.

His mother was the kind of woman who used complaints and criticisms as a sign of love and affection. Chase described her as an emotional whirlwind—she could go from being happy and in a good mood to slamming doors and crying. As a boy she criticized him for his grades, the way he talked, and what he wore, and she would make comments about his body, sometimes shaming him for the way he looked.

"She was hard on me but proud of me at the same time," he said. "It was weird because she would criticize my looks sometimes, but show me off other times. I remember a few years ago she made me drop her at a hair appointment. When we walked into the salon she put her arm around mine and joked with the women that if only she were a few years younger a man like me would make the perfect boyfriend for her. I knew it was a joke, but something about it made my skin crawl."

Chase's mother not only criticized him but judged his wife for her upbringing as she hadn't come from the same level of status that he had. His mother would openly tell him he could have "done better" and would sometimes compare herself to his wife, making comments about how she would take better care of him and his child. In some ways, Chase was more emotionally married to his mother than his actual wife, but he couldn't see it.

Chase had developed an intensely overactive inner critic. He lacked any kind of internal empathy or compassion, and nothing he ever did was ever good enough. His anima, or inner feminine, was mirroring what it was shown. In many ways his inner feminine was an embodiment of his mother—lacking in boundaries, highly judgmental, critical, never satisfied, and prone to extravagant mood swings.

When Chase realized his inner feminine was harsh and resembled his mother, he better understood what needed to be done. He needed to develop self-compassion and learn how to speak to himself with love and encouragement—both things his mother neglected when he was a boy. He began by setting clear boundaries with his mother about what he would and would not tolerate—she was no longer welcome to judge or criticize his wife, and he was going to limit their conversations to once a week. Eventually Chase stopped speaking with her for a few months as he found she was unwilling to respect his boundaries, often testing them or crossing them overtly. She would call him crying and accuse him of being just like his father, which stung deep considering he was trying to forgive his father and find peace with his absence.

But Chase doubled down on cultivating a relationship with his anima. He took up a rigorous daily gratitude practice, grieved the fact that he missed out on much of his childhood, and committed himself to nurturing his own creativity. As he shifted the way he spoke to himself, he became less emotionally volatile, learned to celebrate himself and his accomplishments (of which there were many), and found that his relationship with his wife had dramatically improved as she no longer felt like she needed to be on high alert because of his mood swings.

In order to cultivate a relationship with your anima, you need to be able to get clear on the shadow and impression your mother had on your development.

Here are a few examples of the mother's shadow.

The Overly Close or Enmeshed Mother. She is in all her son's business, needing her son's constant attention emotionally, physically, and relationally. Sometimes this mother can treat her son like a surrogate boyfriend or husband, having him do all the things she wants her partner to do. This kind of mother may have been nosy when you were a boy, snooping through your stuff, asking overly personal questions and constantly needing to know everything about you, or oversharing personal things about herself—because you can't spell *smother* without *mother*.

The Excessively Protective Mother. These mothers usually have a lot of fear and anxiety that becomes the cornerstone of their parenting style. They can be overbearing and prevent you from taking risks as a boy, exaggerating potential risk, using fear to control and maintain closeness. This can create a deep sense of internal anxiety, causing you as a man to fear any kind of risk taking. You may find yourself taking forever to make decisions, constantly weighing the pros and cons, while other times making irrational, wild, and dangerous decisions that have a damaging outcome or impact.

The Neglectful Mother. Maybe because of alcohol or some form of addiction, these mothers can be emotionally disengaged, openly rejecting their children and taking little interest in their child's life. They can be shut down emotionally, secretive, and often have some form of obsession (hoarding, binging TV shows). These mothers can miss out on their son's needs by avoiding physical or emotional connection and lacking any kind of interest in his life, and are usually characterized by a lack of self-care (overconsumption of food, alcohol, gossip, etc.). This can cause a boy to become a man who neglects himself and his own needs, doesn't speak up for himself in his relationships, and lacks the ability to tend to himself.

The Critical and Contemptuous Mother. Nothing is ever good enough for her and she makes sure you know it. Most of the time the only way to get love and affection from her was to perform and meet her expectations. She is critical about everything you do. She can never be wrong, and even in your adult life she is still giving you unwelcome advice while ignoring her own issues. She can be judgmental toward others, hold very rigid and unmoving beliefs, and may be openly offensive toward you or others.

The Wounded Mother. She is the victim. Nothing is her fault, most others are to blame, and she acts as though she can do no wrong. This may be the mother who was depressed and constantly struggled to find her bearings. She emits an ever-present onslaught of negativity, health issues, or grief.

The Saint. She can do no wrong and maybe has never done any wrong in her eyes. She is loving, kind, compassionate, and caring. She takes an interest in your life and does everything she can to love you but makes sure you know how much she's done for you. On some level, you question whether any woman will ever measure up to her.

Maybe you grew up with a very different kind of maternal figure and none of these describe your mother. Regardless of the role your mother played and your relationship to her, knowing the imprint she left on you and your perspective of the feminine is imperative as you develop your own quality of internal worth.

The aim is to fully accept, love, and forgive your mother at all costs, *on your terms.* To let go of your desire to fix, improve, save, and completely relinquish any wish for her to understand you or change in order to appease you.

Look at the relationship you had with your mother as a boy, and the relationship you have with her now. Do you secretly wish you could save her from a failed marriage, or find yourself rejecting her and distancing yourself from her because you don't know how to set boundaries? Was she closed off and cold when you were a boy? Does she still treat you like a child and you allow it? Too many men are caught unconsciously tethered to their mother—not having forgiven her for something she has done, chasing after her approval, or trying to save her from the circumstances of her life. You must be willing to liberate yourself from this dynamic because a man who has not done the work to leave the nest will always be stuck playing the role of the boy, tangled up in the spider's web of their mother's life.

QUESTIONS TO ANSWER ▸ TRUTHS TO UNCOVER

As you go through these questions, take a moment and let yourself connect to the women in your life who impacted your perspective of "the feminine." Let some of the memories and emotions from your childhood, past partnerships, and friendships be present.

Let's start by exploring the person who played the most maternal role in your life, your mother or mother figure.

Women in my family are . . .

Their anger was . . .

Their view of men was . . .

Their relationship to boundaries is . . .

The pain they carried/hid was . . .

I was taught that women should be . . .

The consequences of "breaking the rules" of or with women are . . .

My mother was . . .

I felt neglected by her when . . .

I felt overwhelmed by her when . . .

Her anger was . . .

Her sadness was . . .

I wished she had . . .

Growing up, what I felt like I had to hide from her was . . .

She was critical when . . .

And said things like . . .

This made me feel . . .

I wanted her to support my . . .

Answering these questions has revealed . . .

WHAT YOU LEARNED

Outside of the direct influence your mother had on you is the way your father interacted with your mother. Young boys are heavily influenced by their father's actions and can silently learn how to treat women or relate to the feminine based on the interactions between Mom and Dad.

For a moment, think about how your father treated and interacted with your mother. Was he kind and caring? A pushover who never stood his ground? Was he abusive or aggressive with her, or cut her out entirely? Maybe your father left or was unfaithful. Were you put in a position where you had to protect your mother or wanted to save her?

To get a better picture of this, describe in detail how your father treated your mother. What was their relationship like? How has this impacted the way you treat women, your mother, or the feminine within you? Finally, reflect on how this has informed the way you treat, view, and interact with women.

INTEGRATION EXERCISE

Write a letter to your mom/maternal figure from your younger self expressing what younger you never fully got to say, express, or experience with or around her. Clearly state what you are letting go of and what you will no longer tolerate, look to her for, or engage with in your relationship with her. (Note: This letter isn't to be sent or given to her.)

CHAPTER 6

YOUR RELATIONSHIP TO WOMEN

"Woman always stands just where the man's shadow falls, so that he is only too liable to confuse the two. Then, when he tries to repair this misunderstanding, he overvalues her and believes her the most desirable thing in the world."

CARL JUNG

EVER WONDER WHY you sometimes struggle to get along in your marriage, can't find ease in dating, or feel like understanding and communicating with women is a massive challenge? Maybe you feel afraid of or intimidated by women and get awkward, anxious, or combative around them. Maybe you are constantly seeking their validation or feel totally comfortable in the dating phase, but as soon as things get serious you find yourself shutting down, sabotaging, and unable to communicate your needs while feeling like a failure. While you are certainly not alone, there is a very simple and solid reason for all of this.

The truth is, *the way you treat and view women represents the way you treat your own feminine qualities and unconscious mind.* Think the women you date are overly emotional and chaotic? Maybe you're just as chaotic internally, but most people don't see it. Or maybe you find yourself dating women who are overly assertive, angry, and domineering—a sign of the deep fear you carry about being assertive yourself, and a mirror for your lack of connection to your own anger. In short, women are a mirror reflecting what you are unaware of about yourself as a man.

We as men are so externally focused on the women we are with—what we like or dislike, what we wish would change, whether something could be better—that we miss out on the vital information of *who we become as a man and what is revealed about us in the relationship.*

Often the women you love and are the most attracted to are the same ones you fear. They possess the power to hurt you, make you feel vulnerable, lead you away from your purpose, and sometimes can cause you to feel a certain kind of helplessness. And so, while you may love a woman deeply, pay damn close attention to what it is you fear about her or the relationship—blinding yourself to this can lead to disaster. For example, say you're afraid of your girlfriend's anger and have become resentful toward her about how she operates in disagreements. Rather than setting boundaries and structure around what you won't tolerate during conflict, you shut down, judge her internally, and complain to your friends about her behavior. You view her anger and assertiveness as "the problem," completely missing out on the fact that you're afraid of your own anger and have been disconnected from your own assertiveness.

IT'S NOT ABOUT HER

It's not about figuring her out, trying to change her, solve her, fix things for her, or even "getting" her to like you. *It's about you and what you don't know about yourself that gets revealed when you're around her.* It's about the unconscious insecurities, desires, behaviors, and beliefs that you become aware of when you are in a relationship (or are trying to build one).

Most men are so outwardly focused that they turn their relationship or partner into an object, unintentionally missing out on who they become and what's being revealed—ultimately losing sight of what they truly desire. The woman becomes the object you need to have, the object causing your problems or confusion, or the object that can give you something you need (like validation).

When you adopt this unconscious and almost automatic way of being with women, you become stuck, caged, and imprisoned by the mental model that *what you need to get or understand is outside of yourself.*

And so, you can spend years or even decades running around in circles trying to understand, fix, or solve the puzzle of the women you're with—completely blind to what you are being asked to see, develop, respect, accept, or connect to within yourself.

The key is to wake up in this midst of this externalization. To see how much of your worth, value, attention, focus, energy, wants, needs, and hopes are being projected onto the person you're with or want.

The question isn't, "Is she the right one?" The question is, "How can I better see if I'm being a man I respect when I'm with her?" Only when you are more capable of viewing your own psychology, morals, expectations, boundaries, and needs can you truly assess whether you have found the right person for you.

SHE REVEALS YOUR SHADOW

As Jung said in the quote at the beginning of this chapter, "Woman always stands just where the man's shadow falls, so that he is only too liable to confuse the two." Translation: when we as men lack awareness and focus on the other person, we project our shadow—the good, the bad, the ugly, and the gold—onto our partner, completely missing who we are and what we truly want within the dynamic.

We see all our fears and insecurities in them, become judgmental about the strengths they possess that we feel we lack, or view them as a savior to our missing sense of self-worth. When we do this, we burden both our partner and the relationship while missing out on what we are meant to learn about ourselves.

Take Sean as an example. He found himself in a relationship with a woman he was constantly annoyed by but wouldn't leave. He said she was combative, overly emotional, and constantly irritated him. He became judgmental, was passive-aggressive, and was largely frustrated about the relationship, but he wouldn't leave her—which was very confusing for him.

After working with Sean and his girlfriend, I saw that he was blaming almost all his problems on her and her behavior. He had adopted the mindset that "If only I can get her to change, to be less combative, then maybe I'll be happy." But that was the lie, the fantasy. Sean was upset because he felt incapable of creating order in the relationship, was afraid of being direct, and was scared of asking for his needs to be met—which was a theme throughout the rest of his life.

One day in a session with him, I asked, "What if you had to accept her 100 percent for who she is and there was nothing you could change about her? You could only change yourself and your behavior?"

He paused for a few moments and then said, "Well, I guess I'd have to take a really hard look at why I'm choosing to be with her and why the hell I feel so confronted about having to be assertive and set boundaries."

As we explored what was really making Sean angry about his partner, he described how direct and assertive she could be. When this happened, Sean would retreat, get frustrated and irritated by her, judging her for her supposed lack of compassion.

"I just want her to be more calm, soft, and honestly more agreeable," he said in one of our early sessions. But she couldn't. Not because she wasn't capable, but because Sean was acting like a child, lashing out passive-aggressively, avoiding decisions, shirking responsibility, and acting more like a twelve-year-old than the forty-three-year-old man he was. Sean began to realize that her directness wasn't really an issue—that he appreciated this quality, just not when it was directed at him. He started to see how afraid he was to be assertive, express his own anger or disappointment, and how he felt ashamed that the woman he was with was more direct and clearer than he was.

The problem wasn't that she was assertive; the problem was that Sean lacked assertiveness and had been afraid to develop this aspect of himself. He was convinced that doing so would cause more conflict in the relationship. However, during my next session with them as a couple, I asked Sean's partner how she would feel about him being more assertive. She responded by saying, "Please! Do it! I want a man who can set boundaries. I wish you would just tell me what you want! " Sean looked shocked but excited at the prospect of developing a part of himself he had always seen as a threat.

But that's it, isn't it? *A relationship is meant to teach you about you.*

It's meant to reveal deeper layers of who you are as a man—what you want, desire, will or won't tolerate, and want to build both within yourself and the world. It's meant to reveal what you've been missing about yourself, connect you to your strengths, and show you what you have neglected about your own being as a man. Much like other men can help you hone your skills and deepen your connection to your own masculinity—iron sharpens iron—so too can you sharpen yourself against your relationship.

However, all of this is missed when you're running around like a madman trying to fix, understand, or figure out your partner.

For example, say you lack a deep sense of self-worth and assurance because you haven't developed an internal framework or system of self-recognition. You're harsh and critical with yourself, lacking in compassion, which has become a problem. When you find a woman you want and desire, your lack of self-worth is amplified and you attempt to get her to reaffirm your value. Suddenly you need her to tell you you're good enough in bed, smart enough, or strong enough. You want her to recognize you for your accomplishments, reaffirm your value and worth as a man, and slowly (or quickly) she becomes your singular source of validation. You may find yourself acting needy, harsh, or unreasonable, expecting her to be overly compassionate to fill in for the lack of compassion you feel within. Here, the woman you're with has unconsciously become an object of what you need to develop—self-recognition, compassion, and value. But you can't see this when you're obsessed with her, trying to fix or change her behavior. You must be willing to turn the focus onto yourself and see what she is revealing about you.

After working with thousands of men from around the world, I've noticed a few patterns that this behavior can create. You:

— Become secretly afraid of women

— Pedestal them ("She's so amazing I can't live without her!" "How is she with a man like me?")

— See them as the problem (I wouldn't feel this way if she wasn't so . . .)

— See them as the solution to your problems ("If only she would change, then I . . ." "She could fix this if she only . . ." "I need her in order to feel . . .")

— Become controlling of her actions and behaviors, and try to dictate who she should be

— Find yourself becoming emotionally erratic or volatile

— Degrade/devalue her

— Ignore and avoid women entirely

— Don't trust women and believe they will eventually betray or hurt you

— View women as dangerous, manipulative, and "too much"

— Manipulate them—make them responsible for your decisions

— Blame them for your problems

— Compete with them

The reality is this: *you'll never know what you want in a relationship until you see who you're being in your relationships.* This act of reflection and self-awareness allows you to see the parts of yourself that you have otherwise neglected or never had a chance to develop—your anger, assertiveness, compassion, discipline, self-validation, etc. This is what it looks like to be a self-led man within a relationship—to shift the focus away from what your partner needs to do, fix, or develop, and onto yourself. This doesn't mean you don't have needs or standards; quite the opposite. By getting clear on who you are in the relationship—your faults, strengths, and ability to see what is true—you can more directly articulate your needs and wants while gaining clearer insight about whether you are with the right person.

RECLAIMING YOUR POWER

Your relationship to your partner, friends, work, and the world are all secondary.

Your primary relationship is your relationship with yourself—your choices, ethics, morals, values, and psychology.

Your relationship and partner are a mirror through which to see yourself more clearly—a place to sharpen your edge and develop a healthier, stronger, and deeper relationship with your own nature. Rather than getting caught in the labyrinth of trying to figure out or understand your girlfriend, boyfriend, wife, or partner—trying to control their actions and change how they operate—it's about understanding yourself and controlling your decision-making matrix. It's about understanding your psychological makeup—who you become around them, the way you feel, your choices, what you've been tolerating that's no longer workable, your fears and your desires—while learning to be in relationship with yourself.

She's not the challenge—you are. She's not the problem to figure out—you are. She simply stands at the edge of what you know about yourself but don't want to see or admit, and points to the unknown aspects of who you are and could become. This is a gift.

I see men falling into this trap every day—men who are externally focused on their partner, trying to figure out how to "get it right."

"How can I get them to like me?"

"Why doesn't she want more sex?" Or, "How can I get her to want more sex?"

"We have this same argument over and over. Why won't she just____________ (get over it, forgive me, move on, etc.)."

"If only she would________________ (understand something, change something, see something, validate something, stop or start doing something), then everything would be okay."

Where is the man in all the examples above? Where are his actions, his emotions, choices, morals, and personal psychology? Offloaded onto his partner and the relationship. He has become blinded by the person he is with and largely oblivious to what is being revealed about his own inner nature.

By now you're probably thinking, "I thought you were going to teach me about women, or how to be better with them. How to communicate better, get along better with them, or get laid more." Yes. That is exactly what I'm doing. However, rather than teaching you shoddy tactics to "hack" a woman's behavior or biological desires, I'm bringing you right to the source—yourself. To being the most attractive version of you whether you're single, dating, or married. And how do you do that? Twofold: first by seeing all the meek, insecure, manipulative, and childish behaviors you are unaware of so you can strengthen these aspects of yourself. And second by realizing that when you take all the focus, brain power, time, and strategies you've created to try and understand or be successful with women and apply these to yourself, you become a man who not only knows what he wants but also becomes undeniably attractive to women. When a woman is around a man who knows himself—his desires, wants, needs, mission, and purpose, and who is able to communicate what he needs in a grounded, healthy, and respectful way—she will either have an incredibly deep desire to be with him or run for the hills because she hasn't done the work to be ready for him. Not to mention you will have clarity on whether she is the right woman for you.

Tom, for example, grew up with a critical mother and developed a hostile inner dialogue where he shamed himself constantly. When he got into a relationship with Jenny, a woman he loved and respected, he became needy, continually seeking her validation and praise—looking for the very thing he lacked within. He didn't see his own worth or value as a man and wasn't living in a way that he respected, so he chased after her praise and recognition.

Again, it's not about her. It's about you, your choices, your psychology, and your morals. It's about what you are complicit in creating within the relationship. If you feel like your sex life lacks vibrancy, or the communication between you and your partner is struggling, how are you contributing to the lack of connection or intimacy? Have you become a victim to your partner's moods, or her fear of wanting to engage in sex? Have you let anger and resentment build and brew over months of not acting? What have you been withholding or tolerating? By turning the lens around on yourself, you liberate yourself from the constant and overwhelming number of details you cannot control in the relationship and other person while gaining clarity on what path or direction you can take. You can't change her, but you can change you.

Adam is another good example. He was five years into a marriage and had been acting, in his words, like a grade-A asshole, but didn't really know why. When he and his wife would argue, he would cut her out, not talk to her, and justify being cruel to her, attacking her character. He lacked compassion for her frustrations and refused to acknowledge the pain he was inflicting—something he learned as a child and had carried on not only in his marriage but within himself. He complained about how she was cold and disconnected from him—again projecting his own behavior onto her. One of Adam's biggest complaints was that his wife "always made it about her" and had very little patience for him, when in reality it was Adam who lacked patience and understanding—both for himself and his wife.

For some men their relationship will spotlight how they are lacking in healthy boundaries or discipline. For others it will show their deep lack of compassion, kindness, ease, and connection to their emotions. There is no one-size-fits-all solution other than paying attention to what your beliefs about women are revealing about you.

Payton and his girlfriend had been together for three years. He loved her and could see a bright future with her but wanted a more active sex life and found himself holding off on questions about marriage and children. He had multiple conversations with his girlfriend, Kendra, and found that she was always open to what he wanted to do, explore, and experience. However, Payton was hypercritical of her. He complained constantly about how she tried to initiate sex, how she engaged during sex, and how he wanted something different.

After a few weeks of hearing his complaints about his partner and their sex life, I asked, "What are you trying to change about Kendra that you don't want to admit about yourself? What is this problem revealing about you?"

Payton looked very confused and somewhat upset. Eventually he responded by saying, "I'm not the problem here. She is."

"Okay," I replied, "but what if you're contributing to it? What don't you want to admit?"

He thought for a moment, realizing that I was leading him somewhere.

"Well," he said with a sigh, "honestly, I feel insecure. Everything I've said I want to do and explore, she is willing to do . . . and now I have to act on it, but I don't know where to start. I've been trying to get her to take action when it's me who needs to act."

"Nailed it," I replied. "She's open and willing, but you're scared to lean in and lead. Sometimes our biggest sabotage happens when we are getting exactly what we've desired."

Payton's girlfriend wasn't an issue, and her behavior wasn't a problem—he was unconsciously terrified of leaning into his sexual desires and getting what he had always wanted.

Over the years I've worked with countless men who couldn't decide whether they should stay or leave a relationship. Most of these men talked endlessly about their partner or the relationship, debating whether their partner had the right qualities, acted acceptably during conflict, or whether their sex life met expectations—all valuable questions. However, all of these questions about their partner and the relationship reflected what that man didn't know about himself.

These men aren't struggling to figure out whether to stay or go because they don't know their partner or the relationship—they are struggling because they don't know themselves, which makes the decision nearly impossible.

For a moment, set aside your partner's behavior and any questions you may have about them. Of course, there may be aspects of them or the relationship that you aren't willing to tolerate, but that's for a later conversation.

Start by reversing the lens in your relationship. What don't you want to see or admit about yourself? What decisions, conversations, and actions have you been avoiding? What values have you let slide, and what behaviors have you justified that you know are out of integrity?

As for your partner and the relationship: what stories do you have about them, and what don't you want to accept? Are there certain problems you've been trying to fix? What does this say about you? Can you let go of trying to change your partner, or their decisions, and focus on what you can control about yourself? Sometimes this leads to hard truths and decisions. Realizing that you've been sacrificing your own morals and integrity simply to appease another can be a tough pill to swallow. It's not easy to wake up in a marriage or relationship only to find out it's not *them* you don't respect—it's *you*.

Your relationships to your own nature, psychology, and soul are the most important relationships you'll ever have. When you accept her for who she is without trying to fix or change anything about her, what does it reveal about you? What does it say about how you've been acting—the choices you've made and the boundaries that you've been crossing? And what happens when you shift? Can you use the relationship as a sharpening stone for your masculine nature and let it expand you into a deeper version of yourself rather than it being the cage you need to escape?

Remember, how you treat women is how you treat your unconscious mind and everything you don't know about yourself.

She's not the prize, quest, or adventure—you are.

Begin the journey now.

QUESTIONS TO ANSWER ▸ TRUTHS TO UNCOVER

What I least want to admit about myself in relationships is . . .

What I least want my partner to know is . . .

If they knew this about me, I'm afraid they would . . .

The emotion I least feel comfortable expressing to my partner is . . .

The truth about how I behave during conflict is . . .

The women I usually attract are often . . .

What this says about me is . . .

What I don't want my guy friends to know about my current or past relationship is . . .

What I usually focus on about my partner or women is . . .

I focus on this because . . .

What I'm often trying to figure out about women is . . .

My partner (current/past) says that I'm . . .

The truth about this is . . .

Answering these questions has been . . .

INTEGRATION EXERCISE

So, what's being revealed about you? In order to shift your focus from her or the relationship onto you and your unconscious, there are a few steps you can take to recalibrate.

The goal here is simple:

1) **What's the story?** Define the story you have about your partner (past or present)—is she "too much"? Too emotional? Too aggressive or angry? Too assertive or domineering? Not sexual enough or doesn't enjoy sex as much as you? Pay attention to the things you judge, need, try to change, and dislike about the women you're with—all of this will give you insight.

2) **What's being withheld?** Get clear on the things you withhold from your partner and what you criticize your partner for withholding from you (compassion, empathy, care, recognition, understanding, assertiveness, directness). While some of these things may need to be developed within the relationship, they are also the things you need to learn to give and develop with yourself.

3) **What's being revealed about you?** Are there certain boundaries you need to deploy? Are you being asked to develop assertiveness or self-recognition? Ask yourself, "If this isn't about my partner, what could it be revealing about me?"

YOUR INNER CRITIC

For years my inner critic was abusive. The voice inside my head was vile, corrosive, and wildly demeaning. Anytime I did something wrong, it would immediately attack, lashing out and cutting me down. Learning to confront it and overcome it was one hell of a battle, but one that was deeply rewarding.

At workshops today, I lead men through a very simple exercise: speak to another man the way your inner critic speaks to you when you've done something wrong. This exercise is potent for several reasons, but mostly because the men feel an immediate resistance toward speaking to a brother in that way. "I don't want to talk to him like that, he's a good man," someone always chimes in.

"Then why do you speak to yourself that way?" I reply.

As the exercise continues, the attacks and degrading comments can be heard echoing through the room.

"What the hell is wrong with you?"

"No one else would have fucked that up."

"You're such an idiot."

"You deserve to fail and be alone. You'll never amount to a damn thing and you know it."

For most men, this is not the first time they've heard this kind of slander. The truth is that your inner critic has an origin story. It was created in your formative years and likely has roots in one or many close relationships in your life—a critical mother, an aggressive father who was never satisfied, a school bully, or an over-the-top coach who would verbally rail on you if you so much as looked in his direction. Almost always the voice of your inner critic will sound like the person who you felt was the most critical of you, usually saying much of the exact same commentary. The passive-aggressive jabs that Dad would make, the harsh and cutting commentary from Mom—all of it will show up in the way you criticize yourself.

Some men will have an inner critic that is completely dominant over them—it shows up to shame them for the slightest transgression and berates them into submission, likely carrying on the legacy of a verbally abusive parent or coach.

But what does the inner critic have to do with a man's anima, or feminine?

Well, everything.

The inner critic is the shadow of the feminine. It doesn't use power or force to control you; it uses emotional and psychological warfare to win the battle.

When your inner critic is an overly dominant force within your inner dialogue, it will also incarcerate and incapacitate your more feminine-oriented traits. Things like self-compassion, creativity, self-kindness, emotional expression, and self-recognition will all be held hostage by your inner critic. It is the feminine within you gone rogue and out for blood. It will cut you off from the ability to give yourself grace and empathy when needed and hides the truth of your efforts behind an impenetrable wall of criticism, doubt, confusion, harshness, arrogance, and self-deprecation.

Men who struggle to deploy self-compassion, forgiveness, and empathy for themselves or others are disconnected from their own feminine capacities, and they consequently *need* a woman to provide those things for them. On the other hand, a man can attempt to build his persona in a way where he pretends as though he doesn't need or require any of these things. He becomes disconnected from compassion, emotionally concrete, and often unable to feel the flow and fluidity of life.

How this pattern showed up in my life is straightforward. As a kid I wasn't particularly good at anything—I was average at sports, got along well enough with friends, and was mediocre in academia. However, at some point in high school I started getting attention from women. I found it fun and exhilarating to get their affection, enjoyed winning them over, and quickly found myself shape-shifting into whatever they needed or wanted in order to get their validation. I didn't know how to validate myself because I hadn't found anything I was very good at, plus I had years of being told that I was "useless, a screw up, and will never amount to anything."

I had never developed an internal framework of self-recognition or validation, so when I started getting it from women, it became a drug, something I couldn't get enough of, a kind of emotional heroin I needed to inject daily in order to survive and thrive. I outsourced my worth and value to women, and the harsher my inner critic was, the more attention and reassurance I needed.

The truly hilarious and infuriating part about this whole cycle was, the more attention and validation I needed, the more I disliked myself, and the more fuel my inner critic had to roast me—until I realized that *the validation I was seeking was the validation I needed to give to myself.* It might sound like a simple formula, but it is an incredibly powerful thing to put into action.

Say you are constantly seeking validation from your partner. You want them to tell you how attractive you are, that you're smart, funny, or making the right decisions with your finances or career. Maybe you need them to reassure you constantly and remind you that they are sexually attracted to you because you don't meet your own expectations and criticize yourself after most sexual encounters. This need comes from the insecurity you feel, and even when you get the validation, it's not long before your inner critic has convinced you that it's either untrue or that you must do something more to prove your worth.

The key to breaking free from the inner critic is this: *listen for the grain of truth, develop a framework of self-recognition, challenge the inner critic wherever necessary, and set boundaries with it when needed.* Your inner critic isn't all bad (unless it's being abusive). It's often pointing you *toward* your growth. It illuminates the areas of yourself and your life that aren't working well and need compassion, development, empathy, and acknowledgment.

Spend time each day recognizing and acknowledging yourself for your efforts, achievements, and every time you've met an edge.

Develop a relationship with your anima by challenging and setting boundaries with your inner critic. Be in conversation with this part of you and listen to what might be true while also confronting it when needed. You might hear your inner critic putting you down for something you know you did well and can interrupt the pattern by saying to yourself, "Enough. What you're saying isn't true. I'm not going to debate you because I know I did a damn good job."

Remember, your inner critic is just a pattern: a pattern of doubt, judgment, and criticism that someone else installed in you, and a pattern that you can rewrite.

Do not aim to kill off the critic within, but rather seek to understand it. When was it created? What brought it into being, and how did it gain so much power? Is it carrying on the legacy of someone who tormented you, bullied you, or constantly criticized you? Or did it form as a mechanism of self-punishment and control—a way to make sure you kept yourself in check so you could ensure you pleased someone in your life?

Is it saying something true? Trying to warn you of something? Or is it acting like an overly aggressive and abusive caretaker who needs to be confronted? This may be challenging in the beginning and feel like an overwhelming task, especially if your critic is a result of verbal, physical, or emotional abuse.

When you make an honest mistake, practice forgiving yourself. Be compassionate toward yourself like you would your son, daughter, or partner, and learn the lesson trying to reveal itself. Set limits and boundaries with the critic about what is acceptable and unacceptable.

INTEGRATION EXERCISE

INNER CRITIC ORIGIN STORY: STEP ONE

First, write a list of people who you felt criticized or shamed you when you were growing up. Who were they in relationship to you? As a child, how important was their opinion to you? Rate their importance on a scale of 1 to 10.

For example:

Stepdad – 6

Mom – 8

Bantam hockey coach – 7

Now, write about moments or memories where you remember being criticized or verbally attacked by each individual (or at least the top three). Where were you, what happened, how did you feel, and what did you make the encounter mean about yourself?

INNER CRITIC ORIGIN STORY: STEP TWO

Next, let's explore some of the ways your inner critic began.

Growing up, the person I felt most criticized by was . . .

They said things like . . .

I felt like other people made fun of me for . . .

The parts of me that never felt good enough or accepted were . . .

People in my family criticized me for . . .

Peers at school criticized or made fun of me for . . .

People in authority (teachers/coaches) criticized me for . . .

As a kid, I was hard on myself when . . .

I was critical of my . . .

I was critical of this because . . .

If I (the adult) could say anything to my inner child who was criticized, I'd say . . .

Finally, confront and correct. Don't just take what the inner critic says as gospel; challenge it by asking these three simple questions: *Is it me? Is it true? Is it helpful?*

Is it me? Is this really what I think or believe, or is this someone else's narrative? If it's not me, who is it?

Is it true? Is what the inner critic saying true? Can I challenge it? And how can I know it's unequivocally true? If it's not true, what is or might be true?

Is it helpful? Is what the inner critic saying helpful in some way? If it is helpful, what about it is helpful, and what do I want to do with it? If it's not helpful, what would be helpful?

CHAPTER 7

THE VULNERABILITY MYTH & EMOTIONAL SOVEREIGNTY

"there's a bluebird in my heart that
wants to get out
but I'm too tough for him,
I say, stay in there, I'm not going
to let anybody see
you."

CHARLES BUKOWSKI

MODERN DATING AND relationships have put men in a double bind. On the one hand, men are told they need to be more vulnerable, open up, and talk about their emotions. However, when a man does these things, he can be met with a variety of reactions—anger, confusion, panic, worry, and others' attempts to fix the problems, just to name a few. The reality is that most women still crave strong, assertive, and stable men. And men know this, which leaves deep confusion about how to be strong, stable, and assertive while also being vulnerable, open, and actively showing the soft underbelly of their emotional self.

When you share your feelings, problems, and emotions openly with your partner, she may experience a number of things: she may feel excited and comforted, respond by becoming combative and argumentative, or fall into the maternal role of trying to fix your problems in an effort to help you feel better.

Maybe you've experienced this in one of your relationships. Your partner has been asking for you to open up and share what you've been feeling.

So, one day after work you come home and express your frustration and bitterness toward some of your colleagues or clients and vent about how much you *sometimes* detest your job. Rather than the warm welcome you're expecting, she reacts by reminding you that you need that job and can't quit, or says you complain too much. Maybe she goes into problem-solving mode and provides you with a laundry list of ways you could try to deal with your problem. Either way, you feel frustrated and disappointed by the interaction and bewildered by her repetitive requests for you to open up only to shut you down when you do.

While it is important for you to have a high level of emotional awareness and proficiency in being able to understand and regulate your emotions, simply being vulnerable can lead to chaos and confusion. This is the misconception about men and vulnerability.

THE VULNERABILITY MYTH

The vulnerability myth tells men that if they just open up, share their feelings, and be vulnerable with a woman, then they are a good man—and that somehow, by being vulnerable, most of the issues or problems in their life will be solved. The current cultural narrative tells men that vulnerability is the cure-all for their problems. Is it? Not likely. But can it help sometimes? Of course. Is there a way to do it effectively so you aren't being needy? Absolutely.

And what are women actually saying when they tell you that they want you to be more vulnerable? Let's dig in.

When a woman says she wants you to open up or be more vulnerable, what she is really saying is that *she wants to know that you are aware of your own internal experience and capable of regulating your emotional state*. She wants to be able to validate that you are in some way dealing with the stress, pressures, and chaos of your job, finances, kids, and whatever else you may have on your plate. She doesn't want you to feel like you have to entirely hide what you're going through, she just wants to know what its like as you go through your challenges. Yes, she may want to hear about the details of your distress and frustration, but ultimately what she is looking for is not to solve your problems with you or validate your feelings, but to know that you as a man *are aware of how you are feeling and capable of navigating through it.*

Asking for you to be more open is a way to test how stable you are, how emotionally adept you are as a man. The reason for this is simple: *a man who knows what he is feeling and can navigate through it feels safe and mature and is desirable to a woman.* It is a sign that you will likely be able to handle long-term pressure with work, money, family, or the relationship.

A man who is unaware of his emotional experience, in denial of it, or unable to regulate his emotions when they arise is perceived as a dangerous man, a weak man, a man who is a potential threat to himself, his family, and women.

THE CONUNDRUM OF MALE VULNERABILITY

Here's the double bind countless men, maybe even you, find themselves in: *trying to be strong and emotionally unshakable can be wildly unrealistic or isolating while being open and "vulnerable" can have equally adverse consequences.* Attempting to be emotionally impenetrable can lead to addictive behaviors, depression, and worse. According to the CDC, men (21.7%) were considerably more likely than women (6.6%) to be moderate drinkers and are more likely than women to be heavier drinkers (5.7% and 3.8%, respectively). Also, according to the CDC, males take their own lives at nearly four times the rate of females and represent 77.9% of all suicides.

The reality is that most men self-destruct in silence—much like I did. Most of the time people can see a man is suffering or hurting, but no one really knows what's going on behind the scenes. It's not until after he blows up his marriage, craters his business or career, or burns down his finances that people are let into the emotional dungeon he has been torturing himself in for months and sometimes years. So why not open up and let people in? Why does *being a man* have to come at the cost of shutting people out emotionally?

Well, being emotionally vulnerable, especially around the ones asking for the vulnerability, can be met with rejection, shut-down, and being cast out. There is real risk involved for you as a man to "open up," and you know it. Men may judge you and women may reject you. It's not the cure-all solution it's been presented as by modern-day narratives and often reflects a lack of understanding of the culture we live in. As Brené Brown talks about in her book *Daring Greatly*:

> Here's the painful pattern that emerged from my research with men: We ask them to be vulnerable, we beg them to let us in, and we plead with them to tell us when they're afraid, but the truth is that most women can't stomach it. In those moments when real vulnerability happens in men, most of us recoil with fear and that fear manifests as everything from disappointment to disgust. And men are very smart. They know the risks, and they see the look in our eyes when we're thinking, *C'mon! Pull it together. Man up.*

The harsh reality most women don't want to admit is that many of them do not know how to receive or bear witness to a man's vulnerable side. Some women actively reject it and close off in a relationship, lose sexual attraction, or find themselves less interested and less able to trust after a man expresses his weaknesses or insecurities. Many women say they want men to be more vulnerable, but when a man does express some form of weakness or vulnerability, it can be met with hostility, repulsion, and disgust. So, what are you to do? Hold it in, or let it out? It can feel like a trap either way, which is why we must walk a different path.

OPENING THE CAGE

The challenge you face as a man is knowing and discerning *where, when, and with whom* you can effectively open up. Finding people you respect enough to be transparent with, receive feedback from, and with whom you are willing to reveal the "weaker," less polished sides of yourself will be essential. This can admittedly be frustrating to hear as you may look around in your life and realize there is legitimately no one you would trust in this way. Begin here. Make this your first task and priority. Find the people and groups where the fullest, most robust version of you as a man can be revealed. Join groups like the ManTalks Alliance, find a men's group, and source local events where the kind of men you want to develop alongside would normally visit.

As Charles Bukowski says in his poem "Bluebird,"

> there's a bluebird in my heart that
> wants to get out
> but I'm too tough for him,
> I say,
> stay down, do you want to mess
> me up?

Here, the bluebird represents his softer, gentler side, a part of himself that he believes doesn't have a place in the world. This is the case for some men. They feel this beauty, joy, and gentler side to their nature yet feel unable to let it out into the world, fearing that it will somehow destroy what they have built, or, maybe even worse, be shot dead by the chaos and harshness they are surrounded by.

For other men the challenge they face is that the bluebird is constantly exposed and there is no protection or shelter from the harsh elements of reality. They are run and ruled by their softness, controlled by their emotions, and haven't learned to protect themselves when needed. So, day after day, their sensitivities are picked at, exposed, and rubbed raw by the cruelty of the world we inhabit. These men are directed by their emotions, and vulnerability has become their primary mode of operation, leading to all kinds of chaos and confusion.

Most men oscillate between these two—closed off and stuffed down or exposed and ruled by their emotions, missing out on a third path: emotional sovereignty.

DEVELOP EMOTIONAL SOVEREIGNTY

Emotional sovereignty is about self-governance. It is the capacity and skill of taking complete ownership over one's emotional experience—*to be fully responsible for your emotions while being able to understand and regulate what you're feeling.*

This requires you to feel, not numb.

Claim instead of blame and express, not suppress.

Emotional sovereignty is about being able to see where you're making others responsible for what you are feeling and expecting them to change so you can feel better.

If you constantly need others to change so you feel good, then the dials to your emotions are being turned by them, not you. They say something you don't like, or say it in a certain tone, and you get angry, shut down, or reactive.

Emotional weakness says, "You made me feel this way" or "I don't know why I feel this way, and I wish I didn't." Emotional sovereignty says "I feel this way. It's okay. I am capable of navigating through it, and I have the council to support me."

Emotional sovereignty is about you being in direct contact with your emotions—how they manifest physically and feel in the body, where they come from historically or in the moment, and what they are trying to tell you or teach you. This doesn't mean you should react or decide based solely on your emotions, but they can be valuable data to take into consideration.

However, emotional sovereignty doesn't mean you're alone with your emotions as every sovereign needs a council. As the saying goes, *iron sharpens iron.* The real secret to developing emotional sovereignty is being around men who have a more robust emotional language and stability than you currently possess. Men who are willing to let you vent but are also willing to confront you for complaining about the same thing for weeks on end without doing anything to change your circumstances. Men who can talk about their fears and how they are working to confront them. Men who are willing to discuss the depths of grief after a breakup, death of a parent, or failed business venture. These are the kinds of bonds and relationships most men are deeply craving but admittedly missing—often because they are terrified of the real, confronting, and uncomfortable experiences that will inevitably follow.

And what about revealing your "softer side" to the woman you are with? What does it look like for you to "be vulnerable"? First, you must have built a solid foundation and trust—as I said before, there is such a thing as sharing too much too soon.

Next, build structure. Set the context, content, and direction of what you want to share. For example, if you want to share about a work problem and want to talk about it out loud without getting feedback, you could say, "Babe, I need two minutes to work through a work problem out loud without any feedback. Just want you to listen, can you do that?" Or maybe you need to take ownership over something that you've become aware of with regards to your actions, emotions, or behavior. You may have been feeling grief and sadness about your mother's cancer diagnosis and want to let your partner know what you've been feeling. You could say, "Hey, do you have a few minutes? It's hard for me to say, but I've been feeling a lot of sadness about my mom's diagnosis and just want to share but could also use some insight into what I can do." Again, context, content, and direction.

Let her know what you are doing to work through the challenges you're facing and what resources you've sought out in order to navigate through the obstacles. Share that you are working through this with the men in your life, seeking council, or have found a mentor to help you navigate the hardship, but do not force her to consistently be the person who plays the role of emotional council or emotional mentor.

Worry less about being a vulnerable man and take aim at being a man who is emotionally sovereign.

CONQUERING RELATIONAL CONFLICT: THE RULES OF ENGAGEMENT

Choose a woman you want to navigate hardship and conflict with. Choose someone you are willing to engage in confrontation with and be challenged by. Do not allow yourself to merely tolerate the person you are with and the way they behave during conflict, or this tolerance will lead to resentment and slowly erode the intimacy. Aim to know who they are during conflict and decide for yourself whether this is amicable for you and something you can live with, maybe even come to appreciate.

Contrary to social media memes, relational conflict is not a bad thing. It is a necessary mechanism within an intimate relationship as you and your partner will inevitably have differing opinions, beliefs, desires, and perspectives on how things should be done. If you look at successful and deeply fulfilling long-term relationships, what you are seeing are two people who not only care deeply for one another, but who have become masterful and proficient at settling disputes between the two of them. Now, this may not be what you witnessed growing up. Maybe conflict in your household was volatile, loud, passive-aggressive, or completely hidden altogether. Regardless of the kind of upbringing you had, choosing someone you trust, respect, and know you can engage in conflict with when it arises is crucial.

It may seem unnecessary to say, but a woman's anger and intensity is not an excuse for your reactivity, childish attacks, or volatility. Likely one of your greatest tests within the relationship will be when she is angry, sad, creating conflict, attacking you, or disappointed with you. Stay with her intensity and learn where to create structure or set boundaries. Learn how to navigate her fire and move with the flow of her force, but know where the line is and communicate what you're unwilling to tolerate from a grounded and emotionally calm place.

The ultimate test of a relationship is its ability to hold and navigate differing views, opinions, and desires. How you and your partner engage in conflict will ultimately determine not only your satisfaction within the relationship, but the stability, connection, and intimacy of the relationship itself.

I remember when my wife and I first started dating, we had very different conflict styles—as most couples do. She came from a household where conflict was a kind of love language. Conflict was how she and her father would hash things out. It was how she and her mother engaged on a regular basis, constantly getting in disagreements and misunderstandings. Everything was a battle, negotiation, or litigation process, and in order to get her needs met she needed to fight for them.

I, on the other hand, grew up in a home where conflict was either avoided altogether or was wildly volatile and borderline abusive. I learned how to circumvent conflict, de-escalate people, and became well versed in the skills of conflict avoidance. I also became notorious for provoking people and sparking conflict in my late teens and early twenties, a skill I developed at home and sharpened in my years playing hockey as a defenseman and enforcer.

However, as the relationship progressed and the normal disagreements began to happen, my wife and I would get into conflicts where she fell back into her pattern of trying to argue and pick apart everything I was saying as a means of getting her way. She would take almost everything I was saying at face value, actively looking for any cracks in my argument or words, and attack—almost as if she was defending her case in front of a judge and jury. I must admit that at first I found this to be wildly infuriating, almost to the point of not wanting to engage or "deal" with her in these moments. I would react by becoming louder and more worked up physically, and I found myself back in the kind of conflict I had with my stepfather at an early age—one where I was constantly having to defend myself and ward off any perceived character attacks.

One day we were in New Jersey at her eighty-year-old father's house, and a revelation happened. I watched as my wife began to nitpick at her father—questioning his every word, trying to poke holes through his arguments or comments, and vigorously debating him until he eventually moved on, changed the topic, or completely disengaged. I watched them engaging in an argument that was similar to countless other mini conflicts they'd had in the past and chuckled to myself that none of them ever really got resolved. I found myself thinking back on small disagreements she and I had while pondering what role conflict had played in my previous relationships.

And then it hit me: Neither of us had been taught how to engage in conflict in a healthy, generative way. Neither of us had been taught how to resolve conflict, let alone that conflict could play an important role in our relationship.

On the two-hour drive home, I asked my then girlfriend what role she thought conflict played in intimate relationships. Being one of the top marriage therapists in the world, she said: "Well, conflict is vital for a relationship. It can build connection and intimacy, forming the foundation of the psychospiritual development of both individuals, or tear down the relationship and the people in it."

"And what role do you think conflict has been playing in our relationship?" I asked.

"I don't know. I hadn't really thought about it. But if I had to guess, it's probably been more unproductive than productive," she replied.

We continued our conversation for the next hour or so, discussing what role we wanted conflict to play in our relationship. We both committed to view conflict as another bridge to connection, intimacy, and expansion—as something that would benefit us and the relationship by being resolved.

Later that week I sat down and created the *Conflict Rules of Engagement* for our relationship. These were basic agreements that gave us a foundation where we could engage in conflict, bettering ourselves and the relationship as a result. Some of the agreements were simple, like agreeing to no name calling and taking ownership for what we were experiencing/feeling without finger-pointing or blaming the other person. We both agreed to avoid using universal or absolute words such as *you never* or *you always*, and to assume positive intent. Now we weren't perfect by any means and still fail to live up to these agreements, but they gave both of us and the relationship clear guidelines for navigating arguments.

My challenge for you is to create conflict agreements for your relationship and hold yourself to them. Do not fall into the trap of using the rules or agreements against your partner, but rather lead by example. Create a basic framework for why conflict is relevant and important, how you commit to engaging as a man when conflict arises, and what is unacceptable within the relationship. For example, maybe you grew up in a household where conflict was largely avoided and people were passive-aggressive, never really saying what they meant, or being direct about why they were hurt but using back-handed commentary to tear one another down, openly attacking one another's character. Agreeing to be direct and not resort to passive-aggressive comments may be a solid agreement for you to learn how to resolve conflict more effectively. Because most relationships don't have any structure around how the couple wants to move through conflict, when it arises, they fall back into their childhood patterns, getting locked in unresolved issues that slowly erode trust within the dynamic.

Next, determine what is *cause for a pause* within conflict. You and your partner are not going to get it right or be perfect all the time. Things will likely get heated, someone will break the agreements, and the conversation will fall back into old, familiar patterns. Know the threshold of when you have reached a limit physically or mentally and are no longer capable of engaging in a productive conversation. For most men, when their anger has moved into their heads and they feel a pressure or heat—forehead crunched up, jaw clenched, breath shallow, and thoughts tight or fixated on the other person's behavior and actions—this is a clear sign of being cognitively hijacked. It is a sign that your nervous system and mind have shifted from being capable of clear cognition and into a more fight, flight, or freeze-oriented response, which will almost never produce an outcome of resolution. This is a good place to pause and commit yourself to creating some literal breathing space for yourself and your partner.

Get to know the physical signs that indicate you are cognitively hijacked and need to pause. Do you feel your chest collapsing, hands getting sweaty, or feet wanting to run? Does your breath become shallow and your pulse elevate? Or maybe you become cold and numb, completely shut off from the other person? In these moments, have a set phrase that you can use, like, "I feel shut down and am going to pause this conversation, but will reconnect with you in _______ (20 minutes, an hour, etc.)."

Lastly, to put it bluntly—*don't fight where you fuck*. Commit to leaving conflict out of the bed. Avoid reoccurring arguments and heavy conversations where you and your partner are sexually intimate.

These are all simple yet direct tools to help you lead your relationship through conflict. Use the template in the following integration exercise to create an outline of your conflict agreements.

INTEGRATION EXERCISE

Conflict agreements. If you're single, do this exercise solo and think about the agreements you want for your future relationship. If you're in a relationship, schedule a sit-down with your partner to create your agreements using the following prompts.

1) What I commit to being responsible for when conflict arises in our relationship is . . . (each individual needs to answer)
2) What's off limits for me is . . . (use one word or a short sentence to describe what is not welcome in conflict)
3) I know I need to pause when . . . (describe your cause for a pause)
4) Based on the above, what we agree to as a couple is . . .

Lastly, write out or share with your partner what you *do* like about how they handle conflict.

REPAIR AND RESTORE

If you truly wish to lead within your relationship, then you must be willing to lead the repair. This is essential to emotional sovereignty as you are not waiting for someone else to reconcile so you feel better. This does not mean that you are responsible for solving your partner's emotional problems, but instead means that you dedicate yourself to becoming masterful at moving the two of you through the conflicts that will inevitably arise.

Your commitment to repair will require many things from you. Sometimes it will mean that you must be the first to apologize because you unequivocally know you were in the wrong. Be a man who is competent at apologizing and owning his part of the disconnection. Be direct and clear that you are apologizing without placing blame or responsibility onto your partner. This might sound something like, "I understand I was in the wrong and am sorry for ________ (saying _______ or doing ________)." Other times it will demand that you stay firm and grounded as your partner tests your boundaries or refuses to reconnect after an argument.

There will be moments in your relationship when the connection, communication, or intimacy has been torn. You may find yourself wishing to avoid the conversations necessary to repair the relationship, placing the weight of reconnecting on your partner. Do not get caught in petty internal debates about who is right or wrong, and do not waste your mental or emotional energy closing yourself and waiting for your partner to be the one who creates a bridge or extends an olive branch to repair.

Your work as a man is to protect and maintain that which matters most to you. So, when you disconnect from your partner for long periods of time or refuse to repair when the communication or intimacy has become damaged, you are telling your partner with your actions that the partnership or relationship is not worth maintaining. Eventually your partner will wonder why you chose them, questioning your engagement in the relationship, which can lead to all kinds of issues.

After any kind of conflict happens within your relationship, give yourself time to reground and find your center. No man is capable of being fully grounded or objective when his nervous system is activated and his mind hijacked by the stress hormones released during conflict. Do not rush in to save your partner from their emotions, but instead give yourself time to sift through your own. Often the best thing you can do for your partner is to sort out your own emotional volatility before re-engaging.

Sit in silence and breathe into the intensity of what you feel after conflict has happened between you and your partner. Notice the sensation in the body and what feels familiar. Do you want to shut down and run away like you did in school when the conflict with other kids came knocking? Do you find yourself angry because your partner won't acknowledge you or give you the validation you're looking for? To the best of your ability, stay with the intensity of what you feel without casting blame onto your partner or yourself for the breakdown. Simply return to the sensation in the body—the heat in your chest or face, collapsing in the belly, feet wanting to run or move, hands clenched—and allow yourself to breathe into it. Take two inhales through the nose (first deep into the belly, second into the chest), and a longer exhale through the mouth.

Do this for three to five minutes, keeping your focus and attention on where you feel intensity in the body, letting it expand and contract, slowly dissipating with each exhale. The aim here is to be present to your experience, something you may normally numb or run from during or after conflict.

Once you've regained a sense of regulation and feel centered in the body, ask yourself, "What was my part in this, and how can I repair? What is mine to own, and what is not mine?" This is a good journaling prompt for you to use once you're grounded.

Finally, do not chase, demand, or sulk when trying to repair. Make it clear that you're ready to reconnect and own your part when your partner is ready, but you're not going to force them back into the conversation.

Remember that to restore something is to bring it back into its original state of being, or better. Aim for better.

CHAPTER 8

ILLUMINATING INFIDELITY & PORN

"Affairs are a form of self-discovery, a quest for a new (or a lost) identity. For these seekers, infidelity is less likely to be a symptom of a problem, and is more often described as an expansive experience that involves growth, exploration, and transformation."

ESTHER PEREL

I CHEATED IN virtually every single relationship I was in. Short term, long term, didn't matter. When I was single, I was always seeing multiple women. When I was in a relationship, it didn't take long before I had attracted someone to have sex with on the side. I loved sex; I enjoyed the chase and found myself using sex as a means of celebrating, sabotaging, feeling better, bolstering my self-worth, and numbing out. I had a tremendous amount of shame around my behavior. At the same time, I felt a cold indifference toward my actions, falling into the trap of believing that *once a cheater, always a cheater*. Which I now believe is complete garbage.

I found myself in meaningful relationships with women I deeply cared about but "couldn't stop myself" from indulging in women outside of the relationship. With the rise of social media and dating apps, there didn't seem to be a limit to how many women I could meet, date, sleep with, or have as friends with benefits on the side.

I questioned whether I could have my needs met in a relationship by just one woman—a question I've come to realize many men ask themselves.

Was monogamy really possible for me? Maybe I wasn't built for it? Maybe my sexual orientation was anti-monogamy—whatever the hell that meant. But if that was true, it still didn't explain why I had a profound and intrinsic longing for a committed relationship. I craved the kind of closeness and companionship that a committed relationship often brings. The whole thing was wildly confusing and always left me with more questions than answers.

Years ago, I spoke at a TEDx event and heard one of the other speakers, a sex therapist named Maureen McGrath, say: "Men cheat to stay, women cheat to leave." This sentiment hit home hard as I've heard many men talk about being unfaithful as a means of getting some need or desire met that they didn't think was possible within the territory of their relationship.

When I look back, I can see how in some cases I would withhold my needs and wants from the person I was dating and would stay in a relationship longer than I knew I wanted. But in other relationships, this wasn't the case. Certainly, some men seek out affairs as a means of having specific needs and fantasies met, often needs they don't think they can have satiated in their relationship, but this is not universal. It's not always what's happening.

THE TRUTH ABOUT INFIDELITY

Infidelity is often less about the relationship itself and more about the relationship to the self—to your inner self. The men I have worked with over the years have always found infidelity to be a form of reconciling something within themselves that they have been avoiding, neglecting, fearful of, or having troubles coming to terms with—things they want but haven't asked for or taken action to create, or that they've been tolerating but that have created distance in the relationship. Yes, in most cases infidelity reveals something missing, not functioning, and possibly lacking within the relationship—but look deeper and you will see a man who has contributed to that lack, tolerated it, or left it completely unattended. To be clear, I'm not saying you as a man are solely responsible for all forms of infidelity; I'm saying to pay close attention to what infidelity teaches you about yourself.

Ryan, for example, had been married for a few years and started having an affair after his mother passed away. Her death hit him hard as he had never known his father, leaving him feeling oddly alone in the world. He found himself distracting and numbing out by connecting with women online—using chat rooms, paying for virtual sex, and constantly messaging with women on social media. He became enamored with a younger woman he had been messaging with on social media, which his wife found out about. The shame of the affair broke the dam that was holding back the sadness of losing his mother and the anger of having never known his father—both things he had been bottling up and pretending he was "okay" with but had never truly addressed.

Jarred found himself in an online fling with someone in Europe a year and a half into his relationship. He had never cheated before, but the person he connected with said all the right things and gave him attention in a way that felt intoxicating. He had been largely neglected by his parents, who were workaholics, and found himself in a relationship with a woman who also prioritized work over the relationship. The constant connection with someone, even digitally, had become a high he couldn't resist. Soon he was messaging with multiple people online, and his fling had turned into a separate, secret life.

Danny and his wife had been struggling sexually for years. Danny had been critical of his wife from the beginning of their relationship for not having the same level of desire for sex as he did—which wasn't entirely true, but Danny had convinced himself it was gospel. He had become resentful and angry toward her, rejecting her advances, constantly complaining about her lack of desire, often shutting her down completely—believing the difference between them was irreconcilable. Danny would shut his wife out sexually for weeks and sometimes months, telling her that she wasn't satisfying him while then rejecting her advances.

I had been working with Danny for a month or two when his wife revealed that she had been having an affair on and off for a few months—which she had just ended. Danny was devastated and enraged. At first, he was livid that she would be sexual with someone else yet wasn't satisfied with him. As I worked with them as a couple, Danny began to see the damage caused by years of complaining, criticizing, and rejecting his wife. She described years of desperate attempts to satisfy him sexually—trying to initiate sex on an almost daily basis only to be shut down by him and then criticized for her efforts. Danny, who had been constantly criticized and verbally abused by his mother as a boy, started to see that he had been taking out the rage and grief he felt toward his mother as a boy on his wife as an adult—slowly pushing her away because of his deep fear of intimacy.

Floyd was next in line as CEO of his company. He had worked there for a decade, had a wife and three kids, and had been having an affair with a woman in the office on and off for almost four years. Floyd had been a largely straitlaced guy throughout high school and college, focusing on his career and getting ahead. He had always felt like he had missed out on his "sexual party years" and had had very few partners. His wife, on the other hand, had explored in college and had three or four times as many sexual partners as Floyd, something he was jealous about. He and his wife regularly had sex, but there was something about the power and control he held over the woman he worked with that was wildly exciting. She wanted to be used, and he was happy to oblige her. She would message him to meet her in the janitor's closet after a board meeting, and he got to do whatever he wanted with her. She was married with kids as well but wasn't happy in her marriage. After a few years of the affair, she wanted Floyd to leave his wife, begging him for months, and when he said no—calling off the affair entirely—she filed a sexual harassment claim, bringing Floyd's marriage and career to a halt. Floyd had to reconcile why he would jeopardize everything he loved for an affair with a woman he knew he never wanted to be with romantically.

There are as many reasons why people are unfaithful as there are people who cheat. I've found there is no singular specific rule or reason, but there are a few commonalities that most share.

— Feelings of insecurity or low self-esteem

— Releasing energy/emotion pent up from avoiding conflict

— Feeling caged or disempowered in the relationship

— Differing sexual needs, desires, or drives

— Lack of sexual satisfaction within the primary relationship

— Lack of commitment to the primary relationship

— Differing attitude toward sex outside of marriage that hasn't been communicated

— Lack of emotional connection or satisfaction with the primary relationship

— Seeking escape from financial, family, or work pressures

— The thrill of the chase and a desire for sexual encounters with others

— Curiosity when the opportunity presents itself

Outside of the common reasons for infidelity is the unsavory reality of modern-day relationships. Modern culture and mainstream narratives have burdened relationships and marriage with the obligation of being everything for the individuals within them—leaving countless people acting as if their partner should be everything they could ever need. People in the relationship are expected to be lovers, friends, a life coach to one another, cheerleader, therapist, trusted council, and more. Technology has gamified dating, media has laced marriage with unrealistic, Disney-like expectations, and far too many people skip from one relationship to the next when their partner fails to entertain them or fulfill their unfulfillable expectations. We demonize cheaters, encourage people to vacate a relationship with even a whiff of being unhappy, and livestream people caught in the act of infidelity for some good old public shaming. Cheating has become cheap entertainment, an act of revenge, a cure for boredom, and a way to sabotage or exit a relationship without having the difficult conversation needed to end the relationship.

MOVING INFIDELITY OUT OF THE SHADOWS

I remember sitting next to the last woman I cheated on as she sobbed in the passenger seat while I stared out the windshield of the rental car I was driving. We were on vacation, and it was supposed to be a trip to reconnect and repair our connection as we were nearly a year out from my last "indiscretion." Yet again, she had found text messages and photos from a woman I had slept with in the past. I hadn't physically been unfaithful (this time), but the sexting and naked photos were equally as damaging. As I drove on an empty highway through the stunning tropical jungle of Hawaii, I found myself at an impasse.

Another woman hurt. Another heartbreak, betrayal, and yet another sign that I was still out of control. I remember the distinct feeling in my gut when these conversations would happen. The woman I was dating would find text messages, photos, or other evidence that I was cheating, and my stomach would drop.

"Why can't I change?! Why do I keep doing this shit?!" I would think to myself.

The truth was that a part of me enjoyed it. It was your classic love-hate relationship. I simultaneously felt on top of the world and like the biggest piece of trash.

Infidelity for me was a way to reinforce the story I had been holding for years—the belief that I was broken, bad, wrong, unworthy—while also falsely bolstering my confidence. Most people couldn't see it from the outside, but my inner world was complete chaos. I didn't cheat because I wanted to leave the relationship or because of a lack of sex. I was usually cheating because I disliked myself, and infidelity just happened to be the perfect tool to reinforce the hatred and shame I felt while getting an imaginary, short-lasting injection of self-worth and self-esteem. An odd combination, to say the least.

But, like any good drug or addiction, it gave me the perfect amount of feel-good while dishing out the crack-like dose of shame and pain that I couldn't seem to resist.

I was hurting. Deeply hurting. Sure, the sex was fun, and some of the adventures were memorable. But I was a mess. I felt out of control, lacking integrity, and ultimately alone. Now, maybe infidelity is not your problem and never has been. But surely you have felt this way at some point in your life—out of control, unable to choose the right decision, and spiraling quickly while you grasp desperately for some form of salvation.

The last thing you will want to do is reveal your behavior, and yet you must. Whether to a friend, a counselor, coach, or therapist, acknowledging and exposing the behavior you have buried in the backyard of your life is essential if any change is to occur. Confession is the first step to liberation. Confession is sometimes the only way to pierce through the dam of shame, guilt, and self-hatred we build up when going against our own values and morals as men. Confession and taking ownership for your actions is the steel wool you use to scrub the layers of lies off the surface of your character, which is necessary if you ever want to see what is beneath.

Confession was always the last thing I wanted to do, but the first thing I knew I needed to do in order to change.

I came to realize the simple truth: avoidance makes you weak while ownership develops strength. *Do the hard things, or the hard things do you*—the genuine prison rules of life.

It's not that I wanted to avoid the lies; it's that I wanted to avoid the truth. The truth of my actions, choices, and how I viewed myself.

It may seem obvious to you, and perhaps you read these words with a kind of indifference that I can understand, but this was a real war for me. It was the battle I fought daily. The battle no one had a clue was raging within me. Shame became a black hole within my mind and body that sucked in truth, never to be seen again.

Like Peter Pan, I was a Lost Boy in the world and wanted the comfort of women to distract me from the harsh realities of my life. I felt a vacancy in me that I didn't know how to deal with, and so I poured booze into my belly as often as possible and surrounded myself with the beautiful distraction of women so I could—for a period of time—feign amnesia about how I viewed myself as a man. I wish I could paint a more attractive picture for you, and my ego still wants to make it sound more glamorous than it was, but that too would be a lie.

The reality was I didn't like myself as a man outside of hooking up with women. I didn't have direction or purpose in life; I treated my body like a trash bin and was convinced I was destined for a life of failures and mediocrity. Cheating was a fantasy world where I could escape the shithole of my life. It was an amusement park where, for a brief moment, I could feel *something.* Where I got to feel anything outside of the numb, broken down, and boring state that had become the norm of my waking life.

As Henry David Thoreau said, "The mass of men lead lives of quiet desperation."

I was one of those men. I lived in quiet despair and desperation, and cheating let me believe that I was *doing something* with my life. As if sleeping with countless women would somehow fill the void of living without purpose. Don't get me wrong, it's one thing to date around and be intentional about enjoying an active sex life while building a meaningful existence. But when sex, women, or dating have *become* the way we find meaning in our existence, we will surely be left unsatisfied and unsatiated.

So how did I stop the cycle of cheating? Well, I did the work outlined in this book. But more specifically, I confessed, cleaned the slate, stopped pretending I was a "good guy," and started to work toward being a man I deeply respected.

When we got back from our botched vacation, I did something I hadn't done before. I purged. I went through all my social media counts, deleted and blocked women I knew were tempting, had reconciliation conversations with the women I had led on or cheated with in the past, and chose to come clean with everyone I had been stringing along. I sat down with the men in my life and told them what I had been doing, and made a declaration of what I intended to do to set things straight.

There was no "this time it'll be different" mentality, as I knew this to be an illusion and false story I had bought into countless times before.

Now, regardless of whether you were cheated on or the one being unfaithful, you will need to face some hard truths. Truths about yourself you may not want to admit. Truths about the relationship you've been in, and truths about the person you've been with.

You, too, may need to be molded, shaped, and polished by the rough sandpaper of brutal honesty.

Whether you've cheated or been cheated on, what did it reveal about you? Were you tolerating a lack of sexual connection, afraid to do anything about it? Going along with a life or activities that you genuinely didn't enjoy and so you were looking for some kind of excitement or adventure? Did you allow yourself to act childish, causing conflict and constant fights, pushing the two of you apart until you justified cheating because you feared losing her and were scared to admit that *you* were the problem?

If you let it, infidelity can reveal the kind of relationship you want and the type of sex you've been craving. It will ask you to confront the hidden desires, shame, and loneliness that may have driven you to break your own moral and ethical code. And it can be a chance to define what your ethical code really is as a man. While this might mean the end of the relationship, it could also mean a rebirth of a new and stronger version of it—and you.

PORN

I want to make one thing clear before you read this section: I am genuinely not interested in debating you about porn or your beliefs about it. What follows is not an attempt to convince you of something or get you to believe what I believe. After years of talking about porn with men, I've learned that it is a wildly charged topic, and many men can become defensive, reactive, shut down, or start preaching their beliefs. What follows is based on personal experience, dedicated research, and the experience of the thousands of men I've worked with over the years. If you disagree, great; no problem. If you completely agree, that's fine too. My challenge for you is to keep an open mind and search for something that is genuinely useful to you—not just to reinforce your already established beliefs, but to find something tangible that can shift your relationship to porn, sex, or your own arousal.

I'd also like to confess something: I know I'm biased about porn. How do I know this? Because it has played a massive role in my life. I found it when I was twelve, was watching it almost every day (sometimes for hours) by the time I was fifteen, used it during every single relationship I was in, and spent nearly seventeen years feeling helpless to quit watching it—a theme that some men may understand. Porn was my favorite drug of choice, mostly because I had convinced myself it was harmless—except for the times when I would stay up till 3 a.m. watching it, sabotaging my sleep, health, mindset, school, or work meetings the next morning. Porn was an escape, a mistress, a fantasyland where I could stop thinking about the problems in my finances, career, or relationship. A place where I could feel better, numb out, ignore my stress, feel in control, and a behavior that constantly reinforced the belief that there was "something wrong with me" and that I would never get my shit together.

Now, porn isn't bad or wrong to most people. Maybe for you it's a form of entertainment and a way to get what you want or need in a low-risk, low-effort kind of way. Maybe you never watch it or indulge once in a while with very little worry or concern. You may have found yourself going through periods where you watch it a lot and then drop it completely, or maybe you can't seem to masturbate without it.

Regardless of how often you use porn, I've seen it become the reason why some men don't engage in the kind of sex they want with their wives or girlfriends, the tool some men use when they feel rejected by a woman, and the resource they turn to in order to learn about how they should "perform" in the bedroom. It has also been a resource for some couples to spice things up, try new fantasies, learn about new desires, and gain genuine education from practitioners who specialize in teaching couples how to deepen their sexual connection. So, to say that porn is a complicated topic or subject is an understatement.

With that said, when it comes to us as individual men using porn, I think David Foster Wallace summed it up best when he said:

> Yes, you're performing muscular movements with your hand as you're jerking off. But what you're really doing, I think, is you're running a movie in your head. You're having a fantasy relationship with somebody who is not real . . . strictly to stimulate a neurological response. So as the Internet grows in the next 10, 15 years . . . and virtual reality pornography becomes a reality, we're gonna have to develop some real machinery inside our guts . . . to turn off pure, unalloyed pleasure. Or, I don't know about you, I'm gonna have to leave the planet. 'Cause the technology is just gonna get better and better. And it's gonna get easier and easier . . . and more and more convenient and more and more pleasurable . . . to sit alone with images on a screen . . . given to us by people who do not love us but want our money. And that's fine in low doses, but if it's the basic main staple of your diet, you're gonna die.

I would have to agree with DFW. If porn is the main ingredient of your sexual diet, you will always be left hungry after consuming the empty calories that aim to replace the natural, nutrient-dense sustenance of sexual connection. But this poses a challenge—you need to work and hunt for real-life sex, whereas there is no barrier to acquiring porn. This is the problem for most men: our culture's over-domestication and fast-food mentality have bled into how we pursue sex and companionship. A lot of men have become so fragile, fearful, or frustrated that the idea of approaching a woman in a public place is inconceivable—especially when their favorite OnlyFans girlfriend will, at any time, indulge them in whatever fantasy they want—but it's not free, and it's not real.

The sad truth is that more men are turning to digital sex than ever before. A study done back in 2018 showed that since 2008, the share of men younger than thirty reporting not having any sex since they were eighteen has nearly tripled, to 28 percent, while the number of male virgins has skyrocketed in the past decade from 8 percent in 2008 to 27 percent in 2018—a fairly substantial increase within a decade.

To be clear, there are a multitude of variables playing into this—changes in women's preferences and mate selection, dating apps, fewer men going to college, and the fact that roughly 35 percent of young men between ages eighteen and thirty-four are now more likely to live with a parent than a partner. That said, easy access to virtual sex and pornography has made it easier than ever to opt out of the dating scene and into a virtual world of free or pay-to-play sex.

Maybe you've felt this way in your own life. Finding a partner to date or explore with sexually is confronting. You might be in a relationship and want to explore a specific sexual fantasy or role play but are terrified to ask for it. You don't feel equipped to have the conversation or even question whether it's really something you want because you've only seen it in porn. You want to be bold sexually but feel stifled to take action on what you want and find yourself sitting on the toilet or hiding in your office later that day with thirty-seven tabs open, all playing out some aspect of your sexual desire.

Again, this isn't to demonize porn. It's about being brutally honest about why you're using it, the impact it's having on your sex life, and a reminder that using porn requires zero skill while getting laid and maintaining a thriving sex life requires real skill, effort, consistency, and resiliency. Becoming masterful in the realm of sex requires effort, training, and practice. Much like if you want to be good at a sport or a hobby, you have to put effort into developing the various skills required to be proficient. Sex is no different. It requires different skills in order to make it happen, and make it happen in a way that's beneficial to both you and the other person.

To understand why we use porn—and if you want to break free from it—you need to know some basics about what's happening in your mind and body while you're consuming it.

YOUR BRAIN ON PORN

Porn has been around forever, and for good reason: it taps into some of the most ancient and primal parts of our brain on a fundamental, biological level. So what's the big deal?

Well, porn is what we call *supranormal*, that is, it's beyond the brain's normal amount of input. It's all the mechanical and metabolic aspects of sex amped up to eleven and *minus* most of the natural counterbalances. Basically, this means you get all of the neurochemical and physiological responses and benefits of having sex, but without the inherent risk of having someone there. This means you get to skip anything that could lead to shame, embarrassment, failed expectations, and other undesirable outcomes.

Now, this on its own isn't an issue for our brains. We have developed highly resilient bodies and minds and can handle some wildly supranormal things from time to time. After all, supranormal doesn't mean supernatural. Consuming a Thanksgiving feast is a supranormal dinner, for example. When faced with these occasional events of overconsumption or overstimulation, our entire system works around the clock to balance us out, protect our health, and clear any lasting effects from the sudden change.

However, when something supranormal becomes "the norm," your body responds to the constant stimulation by "downregulating" or lowering your ability to respond. Overeat for two months straight, and you'll develop insulin resistance, gain weight, and your body will struggle to process the abundance of food. You might increasingly be lethargic and have less energy because your body is in a constant state of breaking down more than it can possibly account for. Feast on porn consistently, and (broadly speaking) you'll develop resistance to the neurotransmitters released during sex: dopamine, oxytocin, prolactin, and more.

Dopamine here is the real kicker. There are entire volumes of research and books that outline the role of dopamine. Still, to try and distill it, dopamine is a neuromodulator or a brain chemical that influences the communication of many neurons. It plays a vital role in how you feel as you read this book and affects your levels of motivation and desire, including your willingness to put effort into something and push through the resistance you experience when making any kind of effort. Dopamine is so crucial to your body's functioning that it can even influence how you perceive time.

As Stanford professor of neurobiology Dr. Andrew Huberman has said, "Your level of dopamine is the primary determinant of how motivated we are, how excited we are, how outward-facing we are, and how willing we are to lean into life and pursue things." And as the saying goes, all dopamine wants is more dopamine. It is the molecule of more.

You, right now, have a baseline of dopamine circulating through your body. That level of dopamine may increase or decrease depending on your actions. Now, let's say that you introduce a supranormal experience like watching porn. This can raise, or spike, your baseline level of dopamine, giving you a peak level of dopamine in the body, which will feel good for a while. However, after every peak, there is a crash. After having peak dopamine levels, the residual side-effect is that your normal baseline drops slightly for some time, putting you in a downregulated state.

A growing body of research speaks to the consequences of regularly forcing our brains into this downregulation. Most of it isn't great.

It can impact commitment. In 2012, a study was published in the *Journal of Social and Clinical Psychology*. After studying hundreds of young adult couples, researchers discovered a correlation between hours of porn usage and decreased feelings of commitment toward one's partner. There was a higher tendency among heavy porn users to flirt more often with people outside their relationship, as well as higher incidences of infidelity. Makes sense, considering the findings below.

It affects brain volume. Two years later, in 2014, researchers at the prestigious Max Planck Institute in Berlin discovered "a significant negative association" between reported hours of porn use and brain volume in the right caudate, an ancient part of the brain that helps us learn, set goals, and (get this) navigate *romantic relationships*. In short, there weren't as many neurons to cover those jobs. This is one of the reasons why, if you watch porn frequently, you might find yourself less motivated and more distracted.

It impacts a man's sexual "script." Research has also uncovered that this downregulation changes the way we perceive sex: how it should be, what we need, what our partner needs, what we should look like, and how we should approach it. Said another way, porn rewrites your cognitive playbook.

A study sampling college-age men from across America "showed the more pornography a man watches, the more likely he was to use it during sex, request particular pornographic sex acts of his partner, [and] deliberately conjure images of pornography during sex to maintain arousal." On top of that, they noticed a *negative* association between higher porn use and enjoying sex with each other in couples.

These studies are just the tip of the iceberg with dozens more over the years all pointing to higher incidences of depression, erectile dysfunction, sick leave, and lower overall health.

I want to emphasize that all the studies I read were focused on *heavy* porn use. We're talking every other day, often more. Men who use porn every now and then—to spice things up with a partner or for fun during masturbation, for example—tended to do just fine. Again, our bodies are resilient in the face of some supranormal action.

But overall, the scientific conclusion is that heavy porn use has a significant and negative impact on a man's quality of life through downregulating and diminishing our overall response to pleasure. As far as the brain is concerned, you really can have too much of a good thing.

In tandem with the science, the numbers, and the chemistry is your day-to-day experience.

Porn is an easy way to make sure you get what you want without getting hurt. Googling "lesbian threesome" carries zero risk (unless you forget to turn on incognito mode). The downstream effect of this is that you don't ever have to come into contact with your sexual fear. Fear of intimacy, fear of getting shut down, and even the fear of getting *precisely what you want.*

This means learning to face your fears around intimacy is essential. Otherwise, you run a higher risk of rationalizing why you should use porn again.

OUTGROWING PORN

Okay, so how do you outgrow porn if you've determined that you no longer wish to use it? Well, that's the catch. As many men come to realize, it might not be as easy as you thought because your dopamine system is now wrapped up in the act of watching porn. Some men have used porn for so long to masturbate that they can't remember the last time they got off without it.

Thankfully there are a few tools you can deploy. Below is the strategy I used and countless men I've worked with have practiced with solid results.

First, *start by understanding your porn ritual.* Almost all the men I've worked with over the years have a pattern around their porn use. They watch it at certain times, under specific conditions, and for specific reasons—often going through trends with the type of sexual content they are compelled to consume. Some men watch porn first thing in the morning while others have a habit of viewing it before bed. You might watch it in a particular room or in a specific position (sitting, standing, lying down) and may be surprised at how much of your porn use has become ritualized.

For most men, high stress and failures at work or in their relationships can trigger their desire to watch porn, which can be a part of the ritual. There is almost always a certain emotion or experience that precedes the porn watching—feeling bored, numb, stressed out, anxious, angry, lonely, or disconnected. Yes, sometimes it's because you're just plain horny and turned on, but for the men who have been wanting to quit porn and have struggled to stop, it's always because porn is helping them to avoid pain (disconnection, anxiety, anger, etc.) while delivering the pleasure of relaxation and release. Porn, for some men, has become a way to regulate their emotions, body, and nervous system at the expense of their sexual and intimate relationships.

One man I worked with would wait until his wife was asleep (she went to bed before him) and watch porn in the bathroom upstairs, where he could lock the door. He would often dim the lights and lay a towel out on the floor in case he got tired of sitting on the toilet—a routine he'd had since he was thirteen. As we explored his porn routine, he discovered that on high-stress days and days where he and his wife would argue, the urge to watch porn was much higher, almost unbearable, compared to when they were in a good place relationally. Watching porn had become his form of "self-care," like taking a bath or getting a massage. It was a way for him to feel "connected" to a woman when he was clearly disconnected from the woman he married.

Take a moment to map out your porn ritual. Where, when, why, and how does it happen?

Next, after having a better picture of your porn ritual, *alter this ritual by going on a dopamine fast.* This will mean spending thirty days (minimum) without porn and even, as I've found is quite helpful for many men, not masturbating at all for the duration of the fast. If you are an active viewer of porn, the first seven to ten days will feel damn near impossible. Stick with it. If possible, get an accountability partner or someone you can go through this experience with.

Lastly, *disrupt your porn ritual with a more generative routine.* When you feel the desire to watch porn, make sure you have something to turn to—meditation, breathwork, a creative project, or a physical activity. If you're in a relationship, bring your sexual energy to your partner and engage without expectations or needing a certain outcome to happen. Maybe you make out and feel the intensity of your arousal build, make an advance, or tease your partner to see if you can evoke a response or arousal from them as well.

Now to be honest, this process took me multiple attempts, a whole lot of frustration, and some real dedication to achieve. It might be easier for you, and I sincerely hope it is, but know that this might not be easy. You might be able to not watch porn for 30 days, but find yourself masturbating even more, becoming argumentative and irritable with your partner, friends, or colleagues at work. Stick with it. Practice regulating your nervous system with some of the tools you've learned in this book, working out, breathwork, or dedicating yourself to maintaining a healthy sexual connection with your partner during the 30 days.

Outside of the tactical alterations you can make to your porn usage is the necessary and psychologically confronting component of exploring your sexual desires with your partner. This is something we will cover in depth in a coming chapter.

INTEGRATION EXERCISE

YOUR PORN/VIRTUAL SEX RITUAL

Write out in detail what your porn ritual looks like. Be specific. Include details ranging from where you need to be to what you need to use.

Ask yourself: What do I feel before watching porn? For example, I'm usually feeling __________ (stressed, overwhelmed, anxious, bored, etc.).

Share the ritual with men in your men's group and discuss what you actually need in those moments.

Do a thirty-day "dopamine fast" to reset your system. Restrict porn from your browser and phone, get an accountability partner through a men's group or one of your friends, and be brutally honest about when you want to watch it and what you're experiencing in your life at those moments when you want to watch it. You can also start out by doing a week-long fast or two-week fast, but try and build up to thirty days.

Have a clear and direct protocol for when you want to watch porn, something like: "I will text my accountability partner."

Check in on whether I'm actually aroused or feeling ________ (bored, lonely, sad, angry, anxious, stressed, numb, overwhelmed).

Implement a generative practice. Meditate, do breathwork, take a cold shower, read a book, work out, etc. instead of viewing porn.

Lastly, celebrate your progress. You will need to practice recognizing yourself for the small wins and improvements along the way. The aim is not to beat the crap out of yourself if you slip up or fail; the aim is to reset, celebrate the progress you're making, and refocus on your aim.

CHAPTER 9

SEXUAL FREEDOM

"Sex is full of lies. The body tries to tell the truth. But, it's usually too battered with rules to be heard, and bound with pretenses so it can hardly move. We cripple ourselves with lies."

JIM MORRISON

YOU, LIKE MOST men, probably crave sexual freedom. The freedom to express, explore, and experience. The freedom to choose who you are with, what you do with them, and the sexual expression you wish to embody. One of the main challenges many men feel when it comes to their sexual vitality or sexual energy is the feeling of being overwhelmed. It is not uncommon for a man to feel an abundance of sexual energy and not know what to do with it—to have desires, fantasies, and an amount of sexual energy that can, at times, feel uncontained. It is also not unusual for some men to be entirely disconnected from their sexual body. You may have felt this way with your own sexual desires—trying to limit how much sexual power you feel when you allow yourself to think about sex, and doing your best to be "in control" of your sexual energy. Maybe you've spent years trying to get your premature ejaculation under control, have shame about the size of your penis, or believe that your lack of sexual experience is a problem.

Needless to say, a man's relationship to his own sexual potency says a lot about who he is and the journey he is on.

You may have desires and wants that are considered taboo, or maybe you grew up in a highly religious environment where the topic of sex was limited to procreation and never spoken of otherwise. All the men

I've worked with have had a deep desire to find sexual liberation. They crave freedom from the sexual constraints of their upbringing, the abuse they may have experienced, or the sexually repressed and dull monotony they've fallen into within their long-term relationship.

You may find yourself wanting to be the embodiment of the king in the bedroom, having a partner who worships you and tends to your every whim. You may wish to play with power and sexual dominance or be put into a role of submission and play out fantasies where the power you hold in your day to day is stripped away. Perhaps there are specific fantasies you want to enact, phrases you want to hear, or places and ways you desire to be sexual.

Say you want to rekindle or deepen desire and intensity between you and your partner. You have been together for a few years but have found yourself withholding your sexual cravings and have allowed the vitality of your sexual potency to wither up and become stale. You are hardly interested in sex, and the relationship has become chiefly a friendship. On some level, you've been waiting for your partner to initiate or show more interest as you've felt unwanted sexually. Maybe you've become resentful and convinced that nothing will really change, even though you desperately want it to. The question here is—can *you* be the one to lead the charge back to sexual connection? As research has shown, most women have *responsive arousal*. Essentially this means their sexual arousal happens after some form of stimulation or engagement, whereas men have spontaneous arousal, which can happen out of nowhere, because of a touch, smell, or something we've seen.

Can you pierce through your own frustrations and view your partner as a sexual being again, reconnecting with your passion and fantasies for her? Can you risk rejection and make subtle advances by bringing sensual touch and playfulness back into your interactions? Can you feel the heat of your own arousal in your chest, belly, and groin, letting your desire emanate through your interactions with her? For some men, the resistance to bringing their sexual energy forward will be deeply confronting, while for others being able to direct it and work with it will be the work.

Regardless of the desire, the aim is to understand what sexual freedom looks like for you and bring it forward with your partner—so long as they are willing, wanting, and open to the exploration.

Do not compromise the kind of intimacy and sexual connection you wish to have in your relationship or it will quickly become the cage from which you want to escape. This may be a confronting idea as you may have never explored your desires outside of a web browser, so the notion of telling your partner what you've secretly been desiring for years may feel wildly challenging—but this is the way. You may have also adopted the belief that your partner's disinterest is a constraint in your ability to pursue sexual freedom. And perhaps this is true. You may be in a relationship with someone who genuinely doesn't want to explore sexually, has deep fears around it, or has convinced themselves that "it's just too late." Regardless of the reason or obstacle, you must be willing to prioritize this, not from a needy and entitled place, but from a place of truth and honesty.

However, sexual freedom must be earned. Do not approach this like another box you need to check off on your to-do list, but rather a quest you are embarking on where the journey, outcome, and future are unknown. Learn to be with and revel in this mystery while pressing forward, removing constraints and fears as you go.

INTEGRATION EXERCISE

This week, journal about sexual freedom and your sexual energy using the following prompts.

What does sexual freedom mean to me?

What would it feel like for me to be free sexually?

What do I need to own or confront for this to be possible?

The fantasies, role plays, places, and experiences I want to explore are . . .

My sexual body is . . .

My sexual energy is . . .

I feel overwhelmed by it when . . .

I feel disconnected from it when . . .

If I was sexually free and confident I would . . .

To me, sexual liberation would require me to . . .

STOP TRYING TO TAME THE BEAST—DIRECT IT

My late teens and twenties were basically a blur of injecting myself with sexual morphine. It was a drug I needed daily. There were times when I sat awkwardly in front of a computer watching porn for hours straight, only to have sex with my girlfriend later that night, and weeks during which the door to my bedroom endlessly rotated from the women I was pursuing. That might sound like sexual freedom, but I can assure you I felt trapped, often feeling like a passenger watching the sexual beast who lived within me calling the shots—messaging women, opening endless porn sites, making sexual comments to anyone I found attractive. I can honestly say that I thank the powers that be for the fact that I grew up in the pre-Tinder era.

I lost sleep to have sex and jeopardized my career, relationships, and well-being to get sexual connection. I spent countless hours figuring out how to tame or get a handle on my sex drive and sexual energy. But taming the force I felt within seemed like an impossible task. Nor was it a worthy one.

If you're anything like me, your work is not to try and tame or diminish your sexual desire; it is to learn how to direct it toward your purpose, partner, and desired contributions. At first this will feel incredibly frustrating, mainly because you will feel out of control for a while as your mind yells at you to regain control.

But as I eventually discovered, I wasn't out of control because I was just horny or had too much sexual energy; I was out of control because I was bored. Lost. Alone. Directionless. Stressed. Sad. Without purpose. Lacking discipline. Unable to deal with my own emotional pain and using sex and porn as a means of filling the void I felt within.

Sex and my sexual energy were the salves I used to solve my problems. When I was feeling, experiencing, or facing something I didn't want to deal with (or didn't know how to deal with), my mind and body would shift my focus and attention onto something much more appealing—sex. However, this was clearly a terrible way to deal with life and essentially led to me getting little to nothing done.

I had never learned how to listen to the wisdom of my body and had never developed practices to metabolize, harness, and direct the emotion or sexual energy I had within.

Over time, I learned how to decipher what my body was trying to tell me—was I aroused, or just anxious? Horny or bored? Lonely or turned on? I got into the habit of sitting and meditating for five to ten minutes whenever I felt the urge to watch porn and asked myself the question, "What am I really experiencing right now?" I started to realize that I was undoubtedly aroused a good amount of the time, but more often than not, I was simply using porn or sex as a means of distracting myself from what I was feeling—boredom, stress, uncertainty about what to do, anxiety, anger. Sometimes when the desire to watch porn or text some random woman was extreme, I would sit and do breathwork for fifteen or twenty minutes, write about what I was trying to distract myself from, go for a run, or do yoga. These practices were chosen intentionally to help me better understand what I was truly experiencing and channel the energy in a different direction.

Slowly I began to understand what I needed in those moments. Sometimes my body needed physical exercise or stretching as I had an abundance of energy. Sometimes I felt alone or bored and wasn't aroused at all, so I would message a friend to meet up or stimulate my brain with writing or head out on a photography walk. Other times I needed to find stillness in which to reflect as some vital information about myself was trying to emerge.

Honestly, it was a long and relatively arduous process. I had spent years training myself to use my sexual vitality and arousal as a means of escaping, so to pull apart when I was actually aroused versus when I was trying to escape was a challenging undertaking.

The truth, as I discovered, was that my sex drive was the ultimate distraction from having to face who I was as a man. I didn't have to know myself when all my free time was spent pursuing sexual pleasure.

If you're anything like me, learning to listen to the wisdom of your body and sexual energy will teach you volumes about who you are as a man. But you have to be willing to sit in the fire. To find stillness amid the most intense arousal, consciously redirect the energy and force you feel within, and learn how to satiate that desire without needing the dopamine dump of ejaculating.

One of the most critical questions I started asking myself was, "If porn and masturbation weren't an option right now, what would I be doing?" This question was paramount in my journey because it shifted my consciousness away from, "I need to get off, watch porn, or have a release" to, "What could I do with this energy that would feel equally as good?" For a period, I practiced "no fap" (no masturbation), and then later semen retention, which was an incredible experience and experiment. I quickly found out how much I was turning to sex, porn, and masturbation as a means of regulating my mind and body. Instead, I began to regulate myself and my nervous system not by distracting myself, but by directing my energy, consciously and intentionally, toward other goals, aims, and passions. There was no shortage of sexual energy, and this didn't diminish my sexual connection in my relationship but rather intensified it. I was much more present and grounded, and I found that my sexual energy was easier to direct. I had to learn the difference between being aroused and being bored, lonely, stressed, emotionally low, lost, or anxious—while ending my use of sex as a release from any of those experiences.

So, I kept asking the question, "If porn and masturbation weren't an option right now, what would I be doing?" Then I would go do it. Hiking, biking by the ocean, grabbing a drink with a friend, rock climbing, reading the book I had wanted to dig into for months, working on a hobby or my business, boxing, or doing some stream-of-consciousness writing. Sometimes this meant sitting down with a pen and paper and letting my hand write out what my mind had been thinking or body was feeling—the stress from the week, the disappointment I had felt about a recent failure at work, and the challenges I was experiencing in my relationship.

I used this energy to produce, plan, write, build, and develop the skills and traits I knew I wanted to create. Soon my sexual energy was a welcome force rather than a tiresome foe.

Do not disconnect from your sexual energy in an attempt to tame it. Let yourself connect to the fantasy, lust, and longing you feel. Stay connected to the breath and body when the intensity of your sexual drive is activated and allow that energy to propel you toward your goals, aims, and ambitions.

INTEGRATION EXERCISE

For a week or two (or a month or two), practice no masturbation. Use the question, "If porn and masturbation weren't an option right now, what would I be doing?" Pay attention to when during the day you feel the strongest urge to masturbate, and tune in to what you're feeling—overwhelmed, bored, anxious, angry, or lonely. Ask yourself, "Am I actually aroused, or am I trying to avoid what I'm feeling?"

Make a list of things you want to do or accomplish during this period—books you want to read, hikes you want to experience, courses you want to take, a physical routine, working on a side project or hobby—and commit to directing your energy toward these experiences.

UNDERSTAND YOUR SEXUAL SHADOW

When Matthew came to work with me, it was under the guise of deciding whether to stay or leave the relationship he was in. He had been dating a woman for roughly two years, and she was beginning to question his level of commitment. She frequently asked when he wanted to get married and whether kids were in the picture. Matthew was open to all of those things and could see himself entering into those commitments, yet he felt some apprehension because they had an inconsistent sex life. He was concerned about getting married and falling into the pattern of boring, irregular sex.

At first in our discussions, he focused on his partner's perceived lack of desire, how she wouldn't initiate, and what she was like in bed. But, as we discussed earlier, how you treat your partner is how you treat your unconscious. His focus was fixated on her and was largely unwilling to look at himself.

Eventually, as we moved our discussions away from what he thought his partner lacked and back onto what he was experiencing, Matthew revealed that he loved the woman he was with and was extremely attracted to her but struggled to feel it when it came time to have sex.

"I don't get it," he said in one of our first meetings. "I am really attracted to her. She's my type, I think she's beautiful, but when it comes time to have sex, I feel resistant. When we are having sex, I sometimes check out, need to think about other women or fantasies to stay hard, and occasionally need to think about other sexual experiences I've had so I can finish." A common experience for some men.

As we explored his fears about the relationship, I asked him to describe what his family said about sex, if anyone had talked about it. He gave the standard answer about how no one really said anything and tried to move the conversation forward. I inquired about his first sexual experiences, what they were like, and what he remembered about the encounters.

Matthew sat awkwardly for a while and then began to describe his first sexual experience. He was twelve, and the girl he hooked up with was two years older and a friend of his twin brothers. He described feeling a ton of pressure because he wanted to show off for his older brothers but had no clue what he was doing. Needless to say, the sexual encounter didn't go well.

"I didn't really know how to get the condom on and kept losing my erection. It was frustrating, and she just sat there telling me to hurry up. Eventually, I got it on, but I wasn't really hard enough to do much. I was so nervous that I ended up getting off in the condom before I could even get it in," he said, half chuckling, trying to break the embarrassment with some laughter.

"And then what happened?" I asked.

"What do you mean?" he said, feigning confusion about my question, almost as if he wished there was no follow up.

"What happened after you ejaculated?" I said, making it clear that it was okay to keep going.

"Well, she was angry and called a friend and I got dressed and walked home," he replied.

"And then? Did you tell anyone?" I asked, knowing full well that most young boys aren't going to keep a sexual encounter a secret.

Matthew described his experience of walking home, trying to decide what to say to his brothers. When he got back, he opened the door and they started cheering, asking him how it went. He bragged about how he got laid, which wasn't true, and felt a deep shame. Word eventually got around school, and Matthew was now known as the first guy to have sex in his class.

Now that he seemed a little more comfortable talking about the subject, he continued to tell me about how he had a girlfriend when he was thirteen who wanted to have sex, but the same issue happened with her.

"I had to keep lying. People thought I was this sex champion when in reality I was a complete fraud. Still to this day, my brothers and best friends tell the stories about how I was getting laid before them. We all laugh and joke about it, and I just never knew what to say. I feel like a fraud."

The more we got into Matthew's sexual history, the more shame and embarrassment we discovered. He had finally found a rhythm in his twenties and had multiple partners and sexual encounters that built up confidence. Still, when he got into his current relationship, many of the challenges began. His rational brain couldn't figure out why he loved the woman he was with but was struggling so much sexually.

One day in our session he said, "Maybe it just means that she's not the one, ya know? If I love someone so much and want to be with them, shouldn't it just come naturally?"

Now, this is a common sentiment. The rational brain wants everything to be linear, straightforward, figure-out-able. However, when our shadow steps into the equation, this is hardly ever the case.

Matthew had never told a soul about his failed sexual encounters and still carried a tremendous amount of shame and embarrassment around his past—something that was resurfacing in his current relationship. He felt an oddly similar shame and embarrassment about how he was "performing" sexually, but rather than leave the relationship as he had in the past, he wanted to figure out what was happening as he genuinely wanted to make the relationship work.

As we explored Matthew's past, more stories of sexual confusion, embarrassment, and shame came forward. He continued to share stories that he had never disclosed to anyone. As he did, he found it more accessible and easier to express, explore, and experience the type of sexual connection he desired in his relationship.

Your sexual shadow is developed in moments when you feel ashamed of your sexual abilities or body, when you are directly shamed by others for having a particular desire or aroused by something deemed taboo. It may be a byproduct of living in a household with staunch religious views that demonize the desires you have or a result of the sexual abuse or trauma you experienced.

Travis was caught masturbating by his religious father, who told him that he was going to hell if he didn't stop masturbating. Years later he was in a largely sexless marriage, carried a tremendous amount of sexual shame, and had become tired of having to repress his desires.

Sam had been married to his wife for sixteen years and they had two daughters. He had always been loyal and faithful; however, for the past year and a half he had engaged in an online relationship with another man who lived in Europe. Sam had been aroused by men for as long as he could remember and would often watch gay porn, but he had never told his wife about his fantasies because he thought she would divorce him.

Cole had found porn when he was eleven on his father's computer and had developed an addiction, needing to watch it before bed most nights in order to fall asleep. No one knew, but when he started dating Amanda, it got in the way of their sex life and relationship.

Carl was sexually abused by one of his stepbrothers and couldn't get an erection when his wife was giving him oral sex because it brought back those memories. He had never talked about the sexual trauma he experienced.

Gary had been married to his husband for eight years and had been paying men online for sex for nearly half of their marriage. He liked being in control and was aroused by telling other men what to do, how to act, and what fantasies they should act out for him, but he had always struggled to bring this side of his sexual desires into the bedroom with his partner.

Mark's first girlfriend told him his penis wasn't nearly as big as her ex-boyfriend's and found himself only wanting to date women who told him he was well endowed, even though he never believed it.

Your sexual shadow is whatever you hide from yourself or your partner. It is developed through the rejection, embarrassment, shame, failures, let downs, abuse, and neglect you've experienced and hidden.

You know your sexual shadow is active when you want to express, explore, or experience something but feel unable to do so. You might find yourself with the opportunity to have sex with your wife only to turn it down and watch porn instead, reinforcing your belief that you have a lousy sex life in your marriage. Or maybe you act out sexual fantasies with women online but have a tremendous amount of shame that you can't bring the desires and fantasies you have into the relationship with your partner. You might need sex to look a certain way or have to play out specific fantasies in order to feel aroused, or find yourself becoming incredibly jealous, angry, and sexually needy with your partner and not really knowing why.

The following are signs that your sexual shadow is active.

— You get reactive when you don't get what you want sexually (shutting down, becoming contemptuous, name calling, etc.)

— You hide what you crave sexually because you are embarrassed or ashamed of it

— You sabotage the opportunity to engage in the kind of sexual encounter you desire (can't get hard, shut down, overthink, become overly self-conscious)

— Your partner is to blame for most of the sexual issues in your relationship

— You are convinced your partner can never satisfy your needs sexually, but you stay in the relationship

— You need or use sex to reinforce your own self-worth or self-esteem

— Sex or masturbation helps you escape what you're feeling or feel better about yourself and your life

— You're unable to express what you desire, even though it's clear what you want

— You search out fantasies digitally or in person but can't seem to integrate them into your relationship

— You constantly compare your partner to previous partners or what you've seen online in pornographic content

— You lie about your level of sexual satisfaction

As Matthew and I peeled back the layers of his sexual history, revealing his shame, embarrassment, and regrets, his genuine desire and arousal began to emerge. He found himself more open to initiating with his girlfriend, didn't need to distract himself during sex, and was able to express the kind of fantasies he wanted to experience. He had finally found the courage to explore what he always wanted to do in the bedroom.

As he confronted his sexual shadow, he developed the sexual confidence he had always lacked but deeply wanted.

Be honest, at least with yourself to begin with, about what you hide and least want others to know about you sexually. What do you hide from your partners? What insecurities surface sexually in your relationship, and what fantasies do you act out in your mind or in the porn you watch, but not in your relationship? How do you feel constrained sexually, and what would you like to explore, feel, and experience in sex that you have trouble expressing?

The key here is to bring forward what you would normally hide in a safe relationship with someone you trust.

QUESTIONS TO ANSWER ▸ TRUTHS TO UNCOVER

Growing up, sex was . . .

What my parents/caregivers told me about sex was . . .

Because of this I . . .

One of the most embarrassing sexual experiences I've had was when . . .

After this I . . .

What I hide from my partners (past and present) is . . .

What I've always wanted to explore sexually but have avoided is . . .

I feel embarrassed sexually when . . .

I lack confidence when . . .

Sexually I tell myself I "should" . . .

MOVE PAST THE NEED TO PERFORM

When performance is the only thing that matters to you in the bedroom, you will miss out on the opportunity for sexual intimacy to be a practice for growth, expansion, and deep connection. Focusing on the need to perform can also create all kinds of issues, as roughly 25 percent of men deal with performance anxiety. This anxiety can lead or contribute to premature ejaculation or an inability to ejaculate, problems maintaining an erection, and heightened avoidance of sexual desires.

Say you have started dating someone you are deeply attracted to. You've fantasized about what the sexual encounter might look like, but as time goes on, you feel pressure building to perform. As it sometimes happens, you feel excited yet nervous about the encounter. The more attracted you feel, the more you find yourself thinking about how important it is to impress them sexually. When the time comes and the two of you are engaged sexually, you realize that you can't stop thinking about whether they are enjoying it and how you are doing, and you're critiquing yourself while the encounter is happening.

This is referred to as self-referencing, and it can be a killer for a man's libido. Self-referencing is the mind's way of taking over and fixating on thought when you are feeling overwhelmed by sensation, ashamed, or trying to ward off possible embarrassment. You might notice yourself engaged in foreplay while continually asking yourself if you'll be able to maintain an erection, worried about whether what you just said or did was awkward, and consumed by the process of trying to observe whether you're performing well enough. You might find your attention completely wrapped up with worrying about orgasming too quickly or overthinking before a sexual encounter because you've thought up a linear "game plan" of every move you'll make, position you'll use, and how the climax needs to happen. All of this can contribute to performance anxiety.

This self-referencing causes you to be both the "performer" and the judge adjudicating the performance.

When you are stuck judging your performance, you detach from sensations in the body and focus all your energy and attention on your thoughts. Notice the expectations you have leading up to a sexual encounter and aim for presence over performance. Try maintaining eye contact, staying connected to your breath, and being present to your partner's breathing and movements. The key is to expand your awareness beyond the limited confines of your thoughts before and during intimacy. Breathe deep into the belly, relax the body as much as possible, and expand your awareness so you're present to your partner's enjoyment. All this can help alleviate the constriction and anxiety produced when you are fixated on your performance.

Get clear about the content of your self-referencing. Why are you focused on that specific content? Are you nervous? Excited? Ashamed? Are you trying to ward off embarrassment? Or have you placed your value as a man on your ability to perform sexually—bad performance means you're an inadequate partner?

So, what do you do? Well, begin by understanding that this performance anxiety stems from three main pillars:

1) **Fear of inadequacy.** Do I know what I'm doing, am I competent and capable enough, and can I prove my value sexually?

2) **Fear of rejection.** Will I get turned down—embarrassed, shamed, laughed at, or made fun of for my desires or sexual body or fantasies?

3) **Questioning whether your partner is truly satisfied.** Am I good enough, can I last long enough, and how do I compare to other sexual partners? How can I tell if they are actually satisfied? What if they are faking it or comparing me to someone else?

To move past performance anxiety, you must be willing to do a few things. Start by creating an inner inventory of what's been going on within you regarding sex—are you nervous, stressed, lacking desire, afraid of being rejected, wanting to ask her a specific question, or ashamed to express what you want to explore? Have you been questioning your own performance or her level of satisfaction? Get clear and specific about the internal dialogue impacting the sexual dynamic. If you're in a men's group or have an accountability partner for this book, or a coach, share this with them, and be honest about the insecurity you've been dealing with in the bedroom.

Next, aim to have outcome-less intimacy. This means entering a sexual encounter without the expectation of it going or looking a certain way. It also means letting go of needing to orgasm after a certain duration or needing to produce the world's best porn-star-like performance. I remember at the height of my need to perform, I would watch the clock, tracking when we started having sex, and needed to last for at least an hour or I would feel like a failure. While I thought I was accomplishing something meaningful sexually, I began to realize that I was more focused on the time that had gone by than the experience itself.

But most importantly, breathe. I know it may sound basic or bland, but the point here is simple—let your breath settle your mind and body. When your body is stressed or anxious, you will have a higher likelihood of running into sexual challenges like orgasming quickly or not being able to maintain an erection. Your breath is the stress dial for the body. If it's quick and shallow, your body will respond by moving into a stress response. If it's slow, deep, and calming, your body will settle into a more comfortable state, allowing you to be more present to the experience. Practice inhaling through the nose and exhaling through the mouth. Let the breath drop deep into the body, relaxing your belly and solar plexus while your attention is on the sensation of the experience. If this feels uncomfortable to bring into sex, begin by using this breath practice when you masturbate.

Use the breath to return to the body, to return to sensation, experience, pleasure, your partner, and presence. Sex can be a meditation or a cage where you can't stop thinking, and the breath is your way out of the cage in the moment. Inhale and exhale through your nose and intentionally bring your consciousness or focus back into the body.

REMOVING SEXUAL SHAME

What are your most embarrassing sexual memories and desires, and how have you compensated because of them? I've asked this question to countless groups of men over the years, and it is always wildly revealing to hear the stories they share. Most men are fine sharing their sexual "accomplishments" or conquests, but very few have ever disclosed their sexual embarrassments, shame, or failures—and they pay the price of carrying that shame alone.

For example, Thomas grew up with a single father who was very sexually active. His dad would bring home random women on the weekends and have loud sex while Thomas and his sister watched TV in the living room. Sometimes his father would walk out of the bedroom naked and make comments about how well he had performed, occasionally inquiring about whether Thomas had heard how well his father had pleased the anonymous woman in the bedroom. Sometimes his father would directly tell Thomas that he "had big shoes to fill." It's not uncommon for children to hear their parents having sex, which can bring its own kinds of shame, but this was different.

As Thomas got older and hit puberty, he fantasized about some of the women his father brought home and would occasionally masturbate in his room while he listened to them having sex. As an adult, Thomas was married with his own children. He struggled to feel sexually connected to his wife and felt shame about not being able to please her. She was thrilled with their sex life and communicated this frequently, but Thomas couldn't bring himself to believe it. He was convinced that he was inadequate in some way and had started fantasizing about another man having sex with his wife while he watched or listened. He had tremendous shame around this desire because he sincerely wanted to know that he was enough for his wife.

As we talked about his past, I walked Thomas through a few experiences and exercises to reconnect with the feeling of being in his father's house. Thomas described feeling like he was never enough; his father constantly criticized him and was incredibly harsh on him—something that had transferred into his sexual body. His father's expectations seemed impossible to attain, and Thomas described having a tremendous amount of shame about the times when he would masturbate while listening to his father have sex. Thomas had never told anyone about this. Eventually, we brought his wife into one of our sessions, and Thomas talked about his childhood. He told her about his father's unreachable expectations and about the sexual charge in the household. As he described these things to his wife, she listened with empathy, and after he was done, she paused, gave him a big hug, reminded him how much she loved him, and said, "So you haven't been trying to please me, you've been trying to outperform your father?" Thomas was shocked—he hadn't put the two together until that moment.

Over the next few months, Thomas would continue to bring his desires to his wife and was much more receptive to hearing how sexually satisfied she was with him. He realized that he wanted to feel confident and strong in the bedroom and allowed himself the freedom to explore what that would look like. They enrolled in bondage classes where Thomas got to tie his wife up and did role plays where he was in a more dominant position, and slowly Thomas let go of the notion that he was incapable of satisfying his partner.

Countless men have experiences like this. Shame about their body because they were made fun of as a child, shame about the size of their penis because of constant comments in the locker room, and shame about their performance because of a cheating ex or previous partner who was never satisfied. The list goes on and on.

We need to deal with our sexual shame by exposing it to people we trust and know are willing to work with us to heal. Shame grows in the dark and doesn't want to be exposed to the light of communication and recognition. Shame wants to stay hidden.

If you lack confidence sexually or want to remove the shame surrounding your desires, sit down with a pen and paper and write out all the ways you feel inadequate or struggle sexually. Be honest with yourself as this honesty is the light you shine on the shame. Explore the roots of where the shame may have come from—a religious judgment, lack of experience, childhood teasing or things you saw, friends or teammates making comments about your penis or body, or embarrassing sexual encounters with past partners.

Challenge any belief that you "should" feel or perform a certain way. Often the shame we feel is driven by unrealistic expectations created to protect us from failure, embarrassment, or more shame. Take risks with the right people. As Brené Brown said, "Vulnerability is earned, not guaranteed." This is especially true when it comes to sexual vulnerabilities. Be courageous in bringing forward your sexual fears and distress. If you don't feel comfortable doing this in your relationship, seek out online groups like the ManTalks Alliance where there are men who have done this work and can support you through it. The hard truth about any kind of shame, especially sexual shame, is that it must be shared in order to lose its power.

PART 3

LIBERATE

FREE YOUR MIND & BECOME A SELF-LED MAN

CHAPTER 10

FACING THE FINAL BOSS: THE VICTIM

"Sometimes people don't want to hear the truth because they don't want their illusions destroyed."

FRIEDRICH NIETZSCHE

THERE WAS A time in my life when I believed I was a victim to my own lies. Years and decades of half-truths and embellishing what was happening in my life had crippled my ability to face, or even see, my reality. I felt like a victim to my own choices and circumstances but also felt helpless to create anything different. I constantly complained and judged the people around me, turning them into the problem for how I was feeling or behaving—and I lied. Man did I ever lie my damn face off. I lied directly, I lied by withholding certain details or events, I lied by overexaggerating what had happened, and I lied by changing certain details—often to make me look better, or to convince someone I was a good person. Ironic, I know.

I couldn't face the facts of my life, and nor did I want to. But since I can now, here they are:

Fact: I was a liar.

Fact: I cheated constantly.

Fact: I was watching more porn than the recommended weekly viewing time for TV.

Fact: My finances were a complete disaster.

Fact: I lacked direction and purpose.

Fact: I blamed my girlfriend, government, bosses, friends, and family for my unhappiness.

Fact: I was abusing drugs and alcohol.

Fact: I hated myself, the way I acted, and the way I treated the people I loved.

Fact: No one knew, and I sure as hell didn't want to admit any of it.

I was living in a reality built on a foundation of bullshit. There was no one in my life holding me accountable, calling me out, or reminding me that my path to freedom and liberation rested on my willingness to tell the truth. And so, I didn't. Instead, I actively rejected any kind of support, accountability, or feedback.

If other people didn't know I was lying or playing the victim, then it didn't happen, right?

Wrong. I knew it. And that was the problem.

But this is what the victim archetype does—it tricks you into believing you're helpless, not to blame, and entitled to act like a jackass, only to leave you feeling like shit later because of your actions.

My lies weren't meaningless; they were a maladaptive (a.k.a. unhelpful) coping mechanism designed to keep me safe.

I had learned early on in life that when I screwed up at school, did something wrong at home, messed up in sports, or broke the rules—I got punished. Sometimes that punishment was minor, like being grounded, benched, or having TV taken away, and other times that punishment was being told I was a useless piece of shit who would never amount to anything.

As a nine- or ten-year-old boy, hearing that I was "fucking dumb, an idiot, stupid" or that I "would always be a failure" and was "a constant fuck-up" felt like it broke something in me—like I had been (or was) damaged somehow and couldn't be repaired. I felt defective and like I didn't belong.

Now, being a savvy and attuned kid, I figured out very quickly that if I lied or even withheld certain information, I could sometimes get away with my actions and avoid the harsh and cutting emotional—and occasionally physical—blows that awaited me. Lies became a way to escape from severe punishment. A way of gaining acceptance, being liked and validated, fitting in socially, getting love, and avoiding pain.

In some ways, *lies saved me from feeling like a victim when I was one.*

ORIGINS OF THE VICTIM

We get caught in the victim mindset in our adult life *not* because we are a victim in that moment, but because we were victimized in the past, or we learned it as a survival strategy. The victim mindset isn't something a man wakes up one morning and decides he's going to let run his life or ruin his relationship—it's a response mechanism. A response to being victimized, put in a disempowered position, made to feel weak, small, worthless, or like a complete and total failure. It can be insidious because it can become the identity we use to regain power, get attention and validation, make things easier, and fit in with certain groups.

The victim mindset is learned. It's something you witness in a parent, are taught by a teacher, classmates, teammates, or a past relationship, or something you've seen others use to their benefit socially. You may have seen a parent constantly reject responsibility for their actions, becoming overly defensive whenever they did something wrong. Maybe that parent would get reactive and volatile when they received feedback, or you heard them complain incessantly about how someone else was responsible for their problems. A huge part of how we learn as children is by simply replicating what we see and experience in the environment we inhabit.

Trevor, for example, grew up with a father who would blame his mother for everything. Nothing was ever his father's fault. Ever. The circumstances didn't matter; Trevor's dad simply would not take responsibility for any wrongdoing. As a teenager this infuriated Trevor, yet later in life, as a fifty-two-year-old man with three kids and a marriage about to implode, he was met with the harsh reality that he had unconsciously adopted his father's victim mentality. Nothing was ever Trevor's fault, he was a victim to his wife's emotions or decisions, and he was convinced that his wife, life, or God was out to get him. Nothing he could do would change his circumstances; it was his wife who needed to make the changes in order for him to feel better.

Sammy grew up getting bullied by the kids at school. He had moved from a foreign country in the middle of grade seven and found himself getting teased and beaten up because he looked and spoke differently. He was now in his early thirties and felt deeply confused about what he wanted to do with his life. He was out of shape, angry about his finances, and felt like all the effort he put into his career, personal development, and health was a waste. His inner dialogue was harsh and abusive as he had carried on the emotional and physical bullying. He had become a victim to his own self-talk and was now both the bully and the bullied.

Some men can confront their inner victim. They can see when and where they are offloading responsibility, not wanting to be accountable, and they can own it instantly. They can see it, claim it, and change it. I, on the other hand, was convinced that I couldn't. I needed life to step in, bringing me to rock bottom, before I could really see the only one who could save me was me.

If you want to liberate yourself from the victim mindset, you too will need to know its origin story. Where did you learn to blame others, and who are you blaming in your life today? Who told you or taught you to reject responsibility, constantly complain, or put you in a position of being powerless and helpless? When did you start feeling stuck or believing that it was useless to try?

Look around at your life today and see where you're trying to "get it right" or feel like you're stuck but don't have any control to change things. Maybe you feel like you can "never" get it right with your partner, feel helpless to get their sexual or emotional attention, and are convinced they need to change for you to feel better. Maybe you feel like your partner's complaints, anger, or perceived sexual disinterest are unchangeable, your boss "has it out for you" or you "never seem to catch a break at work." All of this becomes an excuse to not try when things get tough. Notice where and what you are constantly complaining about or feel like you can't change. Be brutally honest about where in your life you have convinced yourself that how you feel is someone else's problem to solve.

Grab a pen and paper and dig into the questions below. Get clear on the origin of your victim mindset and how it shows up in your life today.

INTEGRATION EXERCISE

PAST

Growing up, the people I saw reject responsibility were . . .

When things went wrong, my parents would blame . . .

As a kid I was bullied/abused/outcast/rejected when . . .
(Give a few examples that stand out.)

The person/people I felt helpless around growing up were . . .

The person/people I felt I could never "get it right with" growing up were . . .

This taught me . . .

The belief(s) and behaviors I developed because of this were . . .

I would lie as a kid when . . .

I lied to (get/avoid/belong) . . .

PRESENT

The person/people I blame and criticize the most in my life today are . . .

I blame them for . . .

I don't like to take responsibility when . . .

I lie when . . .

I usually lie about . . .

I lie because . . .

If I'm honest, how I benefit from playing the victim is . . .

What I need to do in those moments instead is . . .

BREAK FREE FROM THE BENEFIT OF THE VICTIM

Much like I was avoiding real accountability and protecting myself by playing the victim, all men benefit in some way by staying in the victim mindset. Some men get to avoid conflict, others sabotage the intimacy they deeply crave while getting to blame their partner, and others will benefit by getting to stay in the superior position of being "right" while looking down on the person they deem as being "wrong."

If you want to break free from the victim mentality, you must be willing to face the fact that playing the victim serves you in some way—and likely not in a way that's good for you and your life.

Here are a few of the "benefits" you get from playing the victim.

- Avoiding responsibility and accountability for your actions
- Believing you have the "right" to complain or not apologize
- Receiving care and false validation from others
- Gaining others' attention and sympathy
- Avoiding feedback since people want to avoid upsetting you
- Increasing the chances of getting what you want because people feel sorry for you
- Not having to deal with difficult situations and bypassing both anger and sadness
- Less is expected of you, and you can get away with taking less responsibility

What do all these examples have in common? In each of them you are playing the role of the victim to avoid something confronting (conflict, responsibility, being in the wrong, failure, etc.), or you get something rewarding (power, validation, sympathy, etc.).

Think about a recent event where you rejected responsibility or blamed someone else for a challenge in your life. Maybe you've found yourself lying to your wife about having to work later hours when in reality you were drinking with friends from work. Perhaps a colleague has given you feedback recently, but you rejected it entirely by saying, "They just don't know what the hell they're talking about." Or maybe you've been avoiding your personal finances as of late, and whenever your partner brings up the topic of money, you immediately become defensive and launch into complaints about how they never appreciate you or see how much you do for them.

How are you benefiting in these moments? What facts and reality are you avoiding? Are you avoiding something confronting, or trying to get something rewarding?

Take some time to journal on the question, "When I am acting like a victim, I am usually trying to avoid ____________ or trying to get ____________."

FROM VICTIM TO VICTOR

Arguably the most challenging aspect of the victim mentality is that it distorts your reality. When you are caught playing the victim, you don't see reality as it is; you see what the victim archetype has created for you. You fail to see your part, don't want to take responsibility, outsource your power, justify lies and half-truths, and largely try to control things you have little to no influence over.

So, how can you liberate yourself from this reality distortion?

Where most men need to begin, where I needed to begin, is to stop lying and start telling the truth.

As René Descartes said, "I think, therefore I am."

When the victim is in charge and you're lying, the statement above becomes, *I lie, therefore I am nothing.*

Lies dissolve your identity and connection to self-respect, self-trust, and the deep knowledge of what you truly want in life. A man who lives and leads with lies can never fully or truly know who he is, what direction he wishes to go, what his purpose is, what his strengths or gifts are, and whether he is with the right intimate partner. How can you ever truly know or trust yourself as a man if your life is built on non-truths? It's an impossibility and a form of insanity—trying to gain clarity by speaking and living falsehoods.

Over the years I did three main things that changed my life and helped me break free from the inner victim. First is a process I call *autocorrecting to tell the truth*, second is *focusing on what you can influence*, and finally *doing an honest audit* of your reality.

These three tools can help you move from victim to victor. To liberate yourself from the distorted and disempowered reality where the victim keeps you captive.

The process of *autocorrecting* is simple but will take both practice and courage. Spend the next week paying close attention to your communication and catch yourself in the middle of withholding, embellishing, or straight-out lying. When you notice yourself altering the facts or withholding the truth, correct yourself immediately. You might say something like, "Actually, that's not right, it's actually" (or "What actually happened was . . ."). Or, when you find yourself lying by withholding information, you can say something like, "I left some details out. Here's what I didn't mention (or wanted to tell you)." Get in the habit of correcting yourself and replacing the lie with the truth. Just like lying can become habitual, so can speaking the truth, and the truth can be an adventure leading far beyond that of the lies we tell.

Next is being able to *gain clarity on what you can and can't control.* Men who try to influence things they can't control will forever be stuck playing the victim. Look at the problems or challenges in your life right now. How much of your time have you honestly spent thinking about and trying to control things you really can't do a damn thing about? Your wife's emotions, your colleague's attitude, the amount of people at the grocery store after work, whether your boss is on time or in a bad mood—the list goes on forever.

The truth is that the things you can genuinely influence are quite small in comparison to all the things you have zero control over. In any given moment or situation in which you feel helpless, overwhelmed, or deeply frustrated, ask yourself, "What can I influence, and what do I not have control over?" Then be honest. Can you control the other person's reaction? No. Their decision? No. Can you influence how you respond and behave? Yes. When you attempt to control things outside your influence, you give away your power. You actively expend energy trying to alter things that ultimately you can't do anything about! Look at the close relationships in your life—your parents, siblings, partner, friends. How much time and frustration have you endured trying to change or control something about them? Probably a lot. See what you can influence in any given moment and double down on it.

Finally, *perform an honest audit* on the state your life, relationship, finances, and career at least once per year, maybe per quarter. While I normally loathe the word *audit*, it simply means *an inspection of individual or organizational accounts.* Most men are so busy judging, criticizing, or ignoring the facts of their life that they can't actually inspect them. Get clear on what the reality of your life looks like without shame or judgment. Be honest regarding how you feel about the facts and focus your commitment on creating direction in the areas that need work. Remember—the victim will want to blame others for the facts of your life or convince you that change will be impossible or too hard, while the victor wants to know what is true so he can make his next move.

Use the templates below to get to know your inner victim and do an honest audit of your life.

INTEGRATION EXERCISE

PART 1: *SEEING THE VICTIM*

Choose one area of your life: relationship, career, health, finances, family.

Next, be honest about where you're being the victim. Write a list of three to five ways you're rejecting responsibility and accountability or blaming other people for your circumstances.

If you're unsure, ask yourself, "Who have I been blaming?" Or, "Who do I feel is against me?"

Be specific about exactly what you need to take responsibility for, listing out who you may need to have a conversation with.

Then, write out a description of what it would look like to act from an empowered place.

Finally, act. Schedule a call, write a letter, and take ownership over your lack of responsibility, maybe even saying that you've been playing the victim.

PART 2: THE HONEST AUDIT

Time to be honest and face the facts. Go through the different areas of your life and inspect where things truly stand. Remember, this isn't about judgment, shame, or trying to solve or fix; it's simply about being honest and inspecting the facts. Below are some example questions, but I encourage you to write out other facts about these areas of your life.

HEALTH

The truth about my body is . . .

The way I treat it is . . .

I respect it when . . .

In the past I've abused it when . . .

The drugs I've taken are . . .

My mental health is . . .

FINANCES/CAREER

My finances are . . . (Be specific—use actual numbers.)

What my bank accounts look like today is . . .

Right now my savings are . . .

And my spending is . . .

Here's where I really am in my career/business . . .

What I'm proud of is . . .

What I do really well is . . .

My strengths are . . .

I struggle with . . .

My leadership skills are . . .

My communication skills are . . .

RELATIONAL

Right now, the state of my relationship is . . .

What I know I contribute to this dynamic is (state both the good and the bad) . . .

Our sex life is . . .

Our communication is . . .

Our connection/intimacy is . . .

The direction we are going as a couple is . . .

PERSONAL/SPIRITUAL

How I feel about God is . . .

The facts about my relationship to God are . . .

My spirituality is . . .

What I don't know or have been questioning is . . .

What I am scared to admit is . . .

Now that you've gone through the *honest audit*, go back and write out how you feel about each section and what action or commitment you'd like to make based on the facts.

CHAPTER 11

EMBRACE YOUR ANGER

"Be angry and do not sin; do not let the sun go down on your anger."

EPHESIANS 4:26

WHEN YOU ARE *not responsible for your anger, the world is forced to be responsible for you.* Anger can be a power you wield for the betterment and development of your life—a sacred force to protect your family, build your path, and sculpt the body you inhabit—or it can be the fire that burns and damages the things you love. Anger is not a problem, but what you do with your anger might be. How you are in relationship with your anger determines its utility.

Unfortunately, most men have a negative and unhealthy relationship with their anger. It's something their mom told them to avoid because she didn't know how to deal with it, something you may have seen your father be consumed by, and a trait that society often judges men for having. However, anger is simply information. Valuable information about when you are hurt, when a boundary has been crossed, and when you are protecting yourself. Learning how to regulate, modulate, and work with the charge of your anger is arguably one of the most valuable skills you can develop.

I thought my anger was a problem for a long time. As a boy and teenager, I got into fights playing hockey, punched holes in the walls of my bedroom, and wasn't afraid to pick fights at school. As a young man I had a ton of rage and can remember drinking with my friends before heading to a club with the sole purpose of looking for a fight. I tried my best to protect the people I loved from my anger, which often led to me holding it in until it came flooding out, leaving me feeling immense shame and regret. When I was out of control, imploding my life and destroying my relationships, my self-directed anger turned into shame and pity. I didn't know how to communicate my anger and resorted to one of two tactics: stuff it down or be consumed by it. Neither left me feeling like I was leading myself with honor or respect.

For most men, anger is the gateway to the other galaxies of emotions. It is the loyal soldier standing guard at the doorway of our grief, joy, sadness, and truth. Anger is the barrier between the man we are and the man we want to be.

YOUR RELATIONSHIP TO ANGER

The first step in understanding and deciphering your anger is to ask yourself what story or belief you hold about anger itself. Is it harmful? Damaging? Overwhelming? Or is it seen as a danger that should be avoided at all costs?

James is an excellent example. His mother told him that an angry man is an abusive man, so he spent years trying to avoid his anger altogether. He disconnected from his anger in his relationships, allowed the women he dated to walk all over him, and carried a deep shame as the anger he couldn't express had become the cage he couldn't escape. His anger was, instead, directed inward at himself, causing him to be a harsh critic, constantly attacking himself internally. A normal narrative playing on repeat in his head was, "What the fuck is wrong with me, why can't I just say something?"

Ted was disconnected from his anger; he thought that *nothing good could come of it.* He struggled to say no to his wife and set boundaries with his kids, and he was constantly frustrated that his life was controlled by other people. The truth was that he was afraid of his anger. He was terrified that if he let it out, it would cause havoc and chaos in his relationships.

Matt found himself enthralled with his anger on a regular basis but felt helpless when it came to dealing with it. When he got angry, he felt out of control and hostile, and he was almost always ashamed of himself afterward. Matt's father was an anger first kind of man: when things didn't go his way, he let everyone around him know about it. Matt had carried on his legacy even though he desperately wanted to be more grounded, understanding, and compassionate.

Nick watched as both of his parents played out a passive-aggressive dance throughout his childhood, causing him to have a quiet, cutting, and contemptuous rage that would intellectually eviscerate his wife and children. He was largely unaware of how angry he actually was and held the story that his wife was the real problem. Her anger was "too much" even though Nick was the one who was almost always angry and frustrated, harboring a deep contempt for the people closest to him.

The truth is that many modern men are frightened by their anger. It is a savage beast within that they have little to no relationship with, but something the people around them are influenced and impacted by daily.

What about you? Are you truly responsible for your anger? Does it have a place in your life, or have you tried to deal with it by locking it away in a dark cavern within your psyche? Does your anger consume you when you argue with your lover, spouse, or coworker? Do you find it impossible to communicate when your anger is present, or have you become so masterful at avoiding it that you don't even know what it would look like for you to get angry?

Before you learn to work with the charge of your anger, start by exploring the story you've been telling about anger and the relationship you've had with it, and how this has influenced your life.

QUESTIONS TO ANSWER ▸ TRUTHS TO UNCOVER

My relationship to anger is . . .

I've always thought that anger is . . .

The impact anger has had on my life is . . .

I hold my anger in when . . .

I let my anger out when . . .

I'm worried that other people think my anger is . . .

If my anger had a voice and could speak to me, it would say . . .

REACTIVITY AS A COMPASS

Your deepest strength and trust in yourself as a man depends on your ability to respond and make decisions. To consciously choose what you wish to say, do, or communicate. However, when you engage with someone in an overly reactive manner, your ability to make sovereign and conscious choices is radically diminished. When you are reactive, you are doing exactly that: reacting to the stimulus—emotions, judgments, opinions, and fears—of another. You lose your sovereignty and act at the whims of some external force. And reactivity isn't just about blowing up or losing your temper. Shutting down, withholding affection and love, making passive-aggressive comments, freezing, avoiding interactions—all are forms of reactivity.

If you want to develop more trust within yourself as a man, you must look closely at your reactivity. It can either be a compass leading you toward a deeper understanding of yourself or the siren song leading you into the rocky shore of victimhood, blame, and childish ignorance.

Are you someone who pretends to be unphased but silently judges the people around you, treating them from this place of judgment? Or are you a man who becomes reactive and angry rather quickly, cutting people down whenever they do something you disapprove of?

After working with countless men, I've come to find that there is nothing quite like an intimate relationship to evoke and activate your reactivity. The people who know you best are also the ones who know how to activate your anger the strongest. They may say or do things that you interpret as being an attack, condescending, or disrespectful. You can find yourself berating them about their actions or internally deciding to ignore them for a few hours. If you want to see your reactivity in action, spend a week observing the nuance of your frustrations, judgments, or anger toward your partner or a work colleague you can't stand.

Your reactivity is a neon sign pointing toward your shadow. It is a signal that you feel inferior, defensive, hurt, disrespected, betrayed, embarrassed, abandoned, neglected, and out of control. Reactivity is a sign that your consciousness and ability to respond have been hijacked or diminished in some regard.

Defensiveness, passive-aggression, feeling hopeless, shutting down, or aggressively criticizing are all examples of reactivity.

The truth about reactivity is that it is not a conscious response. You are not responding from a centered, grounded, sovereign way. You are replying in a pre-conditioned, emotional, and defensive manner, one that often aims to mask what you are thinking or feeling.

Here are a few signs that you are reactive.

— Reacting disproportionately: it's as if something is much bigger or more important than it is

— Hearing yourself say the same things you have in the past, almost like you're on repeat

— Using "absolute" words like "you always," "you never," "you only"

— Feeling a rapid increase in emotional intensity

— Disconnecting from the person you're communicating with

— Feeling no empathy for the person you are being reactive with

— Overdramatizing what you are feeling

— Feeling a strong attachment to being right

The key to working with your reactivity is to catch yourself in the act of being reactive. To wake up to your own unconscious anger, whether you are being passive-aggressive, judgmental, hostile, defensive, or playing the victim, get very familiar with your reactivity and the signs that you are engaging from a reactive place. This means identifying the physical, emotional, mental, and verbal cues that coincide with your reactivity.

You might notice yourself getting tight in the chest or feeling hot in the face when your partner points out that you forgot to take the garbage out or find yourself getting defensive by making excuses for why you forgot.

Outside of catching yourself in the act, noticing the physical signs is a useful tool of creating a pause. As famous Austrian neuroscientist and psychiatrist Viktor Frankl said, "Between stimulus and response is a space. In that space is our power to choose our response. In our response lies our growth and freedom."

When your partner, boss, or colleague does something that ignites your reactivity, pause. Pause before you reply. Pause and reconnect to your breath, letting it clear away the fog of your agitation, and pause so you can collect your consciousness to respond from a more grounded and centered place.

INTEGRATION EXERCISE

Use the five-step method below to work with your reactivity. Catch yourself when you're being reactive and hold yourself accountable, even when you wish to blame or react to the other person.

How to deal with reactivity:

1) Get familiar with the signs (physically, emotionally, mentally, verbally)
2) Pause (even if briefly) and create space before responding so you can determine what you are experiencing
3) Name it out loud ("I am being reactive/feeling reactive/become reactive")
4) Say what you are actually feeling (hurt, disrespected, sad, worried, anxious, abandoned, rejected, embarrassed)
5) Shift attention from cognition to sensation (move the focus from thoughts to physical sensations and reconnect with your breath, deepening the inhale and extending the exhale)

Prompts to work with your reactivity:

I know I'm reactive when . . .

How it feels in my body is . . .

I get defensive when . . .

I am judgmental of others when . . .

I shut down or don't want to respond when . . .

When I'm reactive, I say things like . . .

The behavior I justify is . . .

CHARGE AND INTENSITY

All men carry a certain charge and intensity within them. Our charge can be the thing that propels us to build our business, create powerful art, make passionate love to our partner, and set clear boundaries with people trying to take advantage of us. Our charge can protect, provide, build, and create, or it can destroy, cause pain, confuse, isolate, and humiliate. It's the thing that wakes you up in the morning ready to crush your workout or convinces you to hit snooze a dozen times before you finally drag your ass out of bed.

Let's make a few things clear in order to lay the groundwork for you to work with your charge and internal state more effectively. First, your charge is *your direct felt experience.* Your direct felt experience can be anger, embarrassment, shame, stress, sadness, confusion, loneliness, numbness, emptiness, or any other experience you are having.

Reactivity, as we've talked about, is when the charge of your anger gets out of control, and you act from your anger directly. You communicate and make decisions unconsciously, mostly because you are not in control, and the charge of your anger is in the driver's seat.

Because our rational mind deals in dualities, the main problem we face when experiencing an intense charge—rage, sadness, anxiety, grief, hopelessness, fear, or sexual arousal—is that we deploy one of two methods: shut it down, or act from it.

The problem here is that the binary of either shutting it down or acting on it doesn't teach us how to be with our own internal state, or navigate the intensity of it. When the only options are to shut it down or act on it, we as men lose our freedom of choice and become a slave to our experience (or a slave to avoiding it).

Say you are at home and you have ordered dinner for you and your spouse. She comes in the door with the kids and sees that you ordered Thai food for dinner and makes a frustrated remark: "Thai food? I really didn't want Thai food. I was hoping you'd order some salads." The majority of men will feel a low or medium charge of anger, frustration, shame, or disappointment in the body and either immediately try to shut it down and ignore it or react from it, becoming defensive, attacking, or passive aggressive. You might shut down your charge and need to numb out later by watching porn or having an extra glass of wine, or you act from it and say something you immediately regret.

Or, say you are at a business dinner and are seated next to someone you find incredibly attractive. The more you talk, the more you feel the intensity of your sexual charge building. You can tell they are into you, but it feels inappropriate to make any advances because it's a work event. Maybe you try to shut down your charge, or, if it's become too intense and has overrun your system, you act from it, making a comment or advance that you know is poorly placed, but felt like you couldn't help because the rush and intensity of your charge took over.

The man in both of these examples is not a free man. He is a man shackled by the charge and intensity of his own experience.

Rather than shutting your charge down or immediately reacting from it, there is a third way: working with it. By working with it, we can begin to modulate or regulate our charge—turning down the intensity at times while upping the intensity when needed. As we do this, we are incorporating the valuable information our charge brings while also being more firmly planted in the driver's seat of leading ourselves and our lives.

Start to work with your charge by staying present to your direct experience throughout the day. Check in whenever possible—at work meetings, during a conversation with your boss or spouse, while on the phone with your mother—and label your charge. At first this might feel unnatural or hard to do because you might not be very connected with your own direct experience. That's okay. All the more reason to practice.

Begin by labelling what the charge is—anger, sadness, numbness, loneliness, etc.—along with describing the physical and energetic sensations that accompany the charge.

Understand that every charge has a different feel, energy, and location in the body, and will be different for each man. Some men might feel the charge of their anger as a vibration in the hands and feet, almost as if they need to do something. Others, like myself, might experience their anger as a heat in the belly that can quickly move into the chest, like a fire that consumes the heart. This charge can be mild at first but can quickly expand throughout the body as it becomes more intense.

Do you feel heat, weight, or tingling? Do you experience a shortness of breath, have tension in certain parts of the body, feel contraction, or experience a hollowness or emptiness? Does it feel explosive and expansive, cold and sharp, or defused and cloudy?

Next time you feel aroused or turned on, notice what that charge is like in your body and do your best to describe it. What happens as your arousal becomes more intense? What changes?

And what about the charge of shame or embarrassment? What's it like when you've done something wrong or made a mistake that you wish you could take back? What does that charge feel like in the body, and what happens when it gets more or less intense?

Notice how different charges—anger, arousal, sadness, shame, embarrassment, etc.—are experienced differently in the body.

Lastly, what is the *intensity* of the charge? Intensity is simply the measurement of the charge. How fierce and potent is your charge? How intense is the anger? Is it mild and a dull hum in the background, or is it so loud, severe, and with such an overwhelming magnitude that you can hardly function? Is it low-grade and manageable (say, a 1–4)? Is it intense or beginning to build (4–7), or is it nearing the point of overwhelming your system and becoming hard to handle (8–10)? If it's low-grade or medium, can you be with the intensity while remaining present to the interaction? Or are you noticing yourself acting from the charge because it's become too hot or too intense? If this is the case, you may want to pause the interaction you're in, or take a moment to breathe and practice moving some of the energy you're experiencing down the body and into the ground so you can continue to engage.

Learning to be with your direct experience instead of shutting it down or acting from it is the path to liberation. By learning to work with your charge, you expand your ability to choose how you respond, speak, engage, and decide, and you elevate your ability to feel deeply into the moments that matter most.

INTEGRATION EXERCISE

Practice tuning into your charge throughout the next few days. Make this a conscious practice until it becomes second nature.

Bring your awareness into your body by breathing deeper into your core and belly. Connect to your inner charge and label it. Do you feel the charge of anger? Sadness? Numbness? Stress? Tension? Joy? Happiness? Calm?

Then, tune into how intense that charge is, letting yourself label the intensity.

Lastly, describe the physical and energetic sensations attached to the charge (hot, cold, expanding, contracting, vibrating, restricting, tense, loose, relaxed, hollow, etc.).

Stay in contact with the charge as long as possible without shutting it down or acting from it, and become aware of what happens to the charge over time. Does it increase in intensity or decrease on its own? Is there valuable information that arises by being in contact with your charge (clarity about a decision, action, boundary, etc.)? Notice whatever arises while you are connected to your charge without judgment, shame, or frustration.

WORKING WITH THE CHARGE OF ANGER

If you can work with the charge of your anger, you can work with almost any other charge you will experience. For most men, the two most intense charges they allow themselves to feel are anger and arousal. This doesn't mean that the charge of sadness, joy, shame, grief, or any other experience won't be as present in your life, but many men will come to learn about how to work with their inner charge through the doorway of their anger.

The aim of working with your anger is to see it as something sacred. Something valuable and integral to your life that allows you to be assertive, set boundaries, create order and structure, and tune into what you are and aren't willing to tolerate. When we do this, we make our anger a sacred experience rather than a shameful one.

Sacred anger is the energy of liberation, freedom, and protection. It's the kind of anger that *moves beyond protecting "me" and aims to protect "we."* It illuminates the darkness of your life and directs the force that allows you to create structure with your partner, engage in a difficult conversation with a colleague, and step into confrontation, and it will enable others to feel safe with you. To connect with your sacred anger, you must learn to stop merging with it or disconnecting from it entirely. You must stay present to it, breathing deeply into the experience of what it feels like in the body to be angry—heart pumping, face hot, energy coursing through your arms or legs—while staying grounded and present to the moment.

Sacred anger does not attack, diminish, victimize, or vilify. It is not hostile or cold, it doesn't justify name-calling, and it doesn't use manipulation or shutting someone out as a means of gaining power. It creates structure and order and maintains a depth of connection that is rooted in love. Sacred anger aims to protect the sanctity of your relationship, honors your truth, and creates order where there is chaos.

Sacred anger is being able to feel the heat and energy in the body without allowing it to infiltrate and muddy the waters of your mind or consciousness. Fire in the belly, open skies in your thoughts. Now, that might sound a little woo-woo or ethereal to you, so let's make it tactical.

If you're someone who has trouble accessing their anger, is afraid of it, or feels overwhelmed by it, put yourself in situations where you can give yourself permission to feel it *without merging with it or shutting it down.* Take boxing lessons, Brazilian jiujitsu, or some form of martial arts. Join a men's group and openly state that your mission or intention is to connect to your anger and give yourself permission to experience and express it. Stop looking for "the right time" or "the right way" to express it and lean into the discomfort of letting it out. Start simple by saying, "I'm angry," or "I'm angry, and I can feel the heat of it in my ________ (face, hands, chest, belly, etc.)."

The next time you're in conflict or feel the charge of your anger rising up in your body, practice breathing the energy of your anger back down the body into your belly, keeping your consciousness and awareness in the body and less attached to thought. Feel the intensity of the anger in your gut, chest, arms, and legs while remaining conscious of your breath. Do not disconnect from the intensity or potency of what you feel. Stay with the intensity and recognize where your limit is—your limit being the place where you can no longer work with your anger and are about to be overrun by it. Use the method provided above to connect to your anger and begin to learn how to work with it rather than letting it work you. Bring awareness to the intensity and remain conscious in the midst of it.

This practice is akin to what a boxer or martial arts master will experience when sparring with another practitioner—learning to stay sharp in the heat of the exchange. Learning to stay grounded and not overrun by rage, hopelessness, or anxiety is half the battle when it comes to any situation in which you feel threatened or misunderstood. Practice directing the charge of your anger down to the floor, letting it root you more firmly into the ground so you can remain grounded.

Practice owning and speaking your anger without attacking, shaming, villainizing, or victimizing.

QUESTIONS TO ANSWER ▸ TRUTHS TO UNCOVER

What I've been angry about in my life is . . .

What I've been avoiding getting angry about is . . .

What I've been getting angry about that has made me feel ashamed or out of control is . . .

How I normally avoid my anger is . . .

If I let myself express anger, I'm worried what will happen is . . .

I feel out of control with my anger when . . .

I know I'm acting from my anger when . . .

When I do express my anger, I feel . . .

When I'm angry, what I feel in my body is . . .

Where I feel it the strongest is . . .

What happens to my breath is . . .

If my anger was healthy it would . . .

The concept of sacred anger feels . . .

If I expressed my anger to protect and maintain structure or connection, it would look like . . .

INTEGRATION EXERCISE

GETTING TO SACRED ANGER

1) Identify who or what has activated your reactivity, anger, frustration, hurt. Be specific about why you are reactive.

   Right now I feel ____________________. Who/ what activated me is ____________________.
   I am angry because (why are you actually angry?)____________________.

2) Next, let the anger/rage have a voice, without any filter.

   If my anger/rage had a voice and could let loose without restriction, it would say________________ (write a few sentences).

3) Make your anger sacred.

   If my anger was serving the purpose of connection, respect, and love, it would . . .

4) Get clear on what you need.

   What I will no longer tolerate is . . .

   What I will no longer allow from myself is . . .

   The structure (boundary) I want to create is . . .

   The action I want to take is . . .

   What I know now that I didn't know before is . . .

5) Condense your feelings, boundary, and action into one sentence.

   What I know I feel is ________________, and as a result, the boundary or action I am going to take is ________________.

CHAPTER 12

FREEING YOUR MIND

"True freedom is impossible without a mind made free by discipline."

MORTIMER J. ADLER

FEAR GOVERNS AND shapes the lives of most men. It decides how we interact with women, partners, family, finances, health, and our purpose, and it often constricts our ability to choose what we deem to be most earnest and honest. This happens due to a false equivalency in the minds of men that says, "If and when I show fear, I will be showing that I am less of a man." Because of this, countless men are afraid of being seen as afraid and end up designing their lives around the pillar of fear avoidance. However, *not showing your fear and not knowing your fear are two wildly different things, with dramatically different consequences.*

The majority of men in today's culture do not know the fear they live with, or what fear itself has to offer. This blindness cripples us as men and cuts us off from natural opportunities to expand ourselves psychologically, physically, and spiritually.

The truth is that a man who is willing to confront and face his fear is of great value to both himself and the group or community he inhabits. To face your fear of rejection, failure, public ridicule, and possible embarrassment not only acts as an example for others, but it's also instrumental for pushing through the natural barriers that stop most people from taking bold risks and life-altering actions. Individual and collective acts of facing fear lead to innovation, ingenuity, social coherence, and all kinds of progress in every area of life—individual, technological, scientific, communal, and spiritual.

Think about any new relationship, scientific idea, or business idea—all required a certain amount of risk that puts one in direct contact with their fears. Maybe you've seen this in your own life where you were afraid to approach a woman and strike up a conversation or ask for her number, only to have it work out better than expected.

However, not knowing, much less facing, your individual fears in today's culture and world is made easy. Modernity and the over-prioritization of safety has restricted the opportunity for men to confront their fears and prove their courage. This, coupled with the constant inundation of the "crisis culture" we are steeped in, often leaves men asleep at the wheel of their own fears while constantly ruminating over and getting overwhelmed by the existential fears of the collective. No longer are men encouraged to venture out beyond the safe and comfortable territory of their couch, office, and routine, but instead are lulled into a false sense of security by never having to endure anything that could potentially be psychologically, physically, and spiritually terrifying.

Fear has become the most well-used tool in the distraction and domestication of modern men.

Don't agree with the social narrative? Don't say anything or you'll be publicly shamed and cancelled.

Don't like what your girlfriend, wife, or partner just did? Don't say anything because it'll lead to an argument, or worse, they'll leave you.

Want to pursue a goal, but know other people will judge you or potentially ridicule you? Don't bother—it's not worth the hassle and possibility of failure.

In your relationships, fear restricts your ability to remain connected to your partner. Maybe you're afraid to disappoint your wife, so you never stand up to her or set boundaries. Perhaps you agree to everything she wants to do, which builds a tremendous amount of resentment within you and the relationship. You might be deeply terrified of being rejected sexually, so you avoid any conversation and interaction that could lead to having your sexual desires met. Or maybe, at your core, you're afraid of being loved, so you sabotage your partner's attempts at getting close to you on any level. Whatever the challenge you're facing in your current or past relationship, you can be sure that fear is somewhere behind the curtain pulling the strings of your actions. "What if they leave?" "What if I hurt them again?" "I don't know how I'll live without them!" "What if they are having an affair?" The list goes on and on.

Fear stands between you and the kind of life you want to lead. It is the bridge that leads you closer to the man you can become. As Jung reminds us, "No tree, it is said, can reach to heaven unless its roots reach down to hell." If you wish to grow, expand, change, or find freedom as a man, your journey will take you through the caverns of your fears.

FREEDOM IN FEAR

I was intensely afraid of not being liked or accepted. As a kid, I found safety and acceptance in getting other people to laugh or open up to me. I didn't know how to fit in, had an incredibly low self-image, and didn't think that people would like me for who I was. So, I got very good at getting people's attention and spent much of my time and energy trying to gain their approval and validation. Eventually it became a drug. I was terrified of not being good enough or smart enough and needed to seek approval and validation as a means of believing that I "fit in." After my life collapsed and I began to rebuild, I found myself confronting the fear of not being liked every single time I told the truth about what had been happening behind the scenes of my life. The lies, the cheating, the substance abuse: I owned it all. Honesty became the steel wool scrubbing away the fear of not being liked.

Over the years I have sat and listened to thousands of men share their fears.

Men afraid to take risks, step out of their comfort zone, and pursue their ambitions. Men afraid to confront the demons within or terrified of the backlash that comes when owning one's truth. Men afraid of dying without having fully lived or felt connected to a sense of purpose, terrified to own their strength, possibility, and potential, and men afraid of having a past mistake, trauma, or abuse play itself out again.

These fears aren't a problem. Your fears are not an issue. How you deal with them might be.

There is no cure for fear. No five-step program you can sign up for or course you can take in eradicating it. No amount of psychedelics, therapy, or thrill-seeking sports are going to eradicate your fear. There is only the conscious act of being aware of your fear, moving toward it, and understanding it. You sharpen the edges of your masculine core by moving toward the things you're afraid of. Having hard conversations, loving more deeply, being straightforward about your beliefs, and pursuing your aims or purpose in life will all bring fear to knock at the door of your psyche. Let it knock, brother. Let it knock, and welcome it in.

Choose an area of your life where you've felt stuck or limited. Maybe it's your career, relationship, health, spiritual practice, or sex life. Take your career, job, or business as an example. What fears do you hold in this area of your life, and how do these fears restrict you from making more money or having a greater impact on your clients or the people you work with? What fears prevent you from leaning more fully into the impact you want to have in your work, community, and world at large? Are you afraid of giving up the security and safety you've built? Worried about what your parents, friends, or partner might say? Maybe you're so afraid to act that you find yourself confused about what you even want. Regardless of what you're afraid of, fear is the place where you settle, become complacent, and relinquish your connection to the fire within.

You may be very aware of your fears and feel overwhelmed by them. You worry constantly about whether you're doing enough or live in fear wondering when things are going to fall apart. Fear has become the main program you operate, and you don't know what life would look like without it. Or maybe you're completely ignorant of your fears. You pretend to fear nothing and live in the dark of the fear you carry about death, fatherhood, or not earning and saving enough money. You pretend like you fear nothing, but your partner, friends, and family can all feel the truth—you're scared but don't want to see it.

Come back to the area of your life where you feel stuck, limited, or complacent. If you tune in deeply to the fear you have in that part of your life, what is it? Write it down in as much detail as you can. To the best of your ability, locate where this fear came from. What does it feel familiar to, and where did it originate? As poet David Whyte said, "It is not the thing you fear that you must deal with: it is the mother of the thing you fear." It is often the thing that birthed our fears that we are contending with—the bullying, abuse, loneliness, childhood neglect, betrayal, or embarrassment we experienced in the past.

Maybe your fear sounds something like, "I am terrified of starting my own business. I know I have the skills, knowledge, and connections to make it happen, but I'd rather play it safe. I know I could take the risk, but I might fail and let down everyone who relies on me. I'm too (old, young, fat, stupid)_________, and should have started __________ (ten years ago, last year, etc.). I don't want to put in the effort. I'd have to have to give up some comforts, and I would rather hide from what I know I want than possibly fail trying."

Respect your fears. Stay close to them, but not so close you merge with them and act from them. This is the key—to stay awake and aware to the presence of your fears while not backing down from them. Get to know them: where they came from, what they want, what they are trying to teach you, and what action or direction you can choose as a result of their existence. Can you move toward them consciously every day, without letting them consume you? A man who is willing to venture into his fears without needing to run from them or force them into submission is a man who will find freedom where others are shackled.

FREEDOM IN ACCOUNTABILITY

Men expand with accountability and contract without it. If you want to integrate anything in your life, free your mind, or develop yourself in almost any way, the men you surround yourself with will be instrumental to your success. Unfortunately, most men have become so fearful of being seen as weak or a failure that they avoid holding themselves accountable or being held accountable by others.

Too many men have become fragile and lack the willingness to have other men reflect back where they are falling short or could be doing better. They surround themselves with men who have the same feeble level of ambition and wonder why they constantly feel weighed down by life and the smallness of their accomplishments, all while wishing for more. Men crave to get the most from themselves and dream about actualizing their potential but aren't willing to put themselves in the vice grip of accountability. When a man lacks accountability in his life or rejects the accountability that shows up, he will contract. Slowly over time he will shrink in his confidence, effectiveness, and capacities. He will become more convinced that he doesn't need help or advice and will view his own opinion as superior to all those around him. This is a recipe for disaster.

Notice how you normally react when someone holds you accountable—your partner, boss, colleague, or friend. Say you missed a deadline or forgot to send an email to a client, and your coworker checks to see if it got done as they are working alongside you on the project. Immediately you get reactive, snapping back and telling them to focus on their own work. You open your email, send the message, and carry on with your day.

Now imagine this happening repeatedly. What is the likelihood of that person continuing to help you be accountable in your actions? Likely not much. They will stop checking in, and things will start to slide on your end. You miss deadlines, don't call your clients when you say you will, and because there is no accountability—no one holding you responsible—it turns into a much larger issue. Maybe your boss intervenes at some point and has a "performance" conversation with you, or you miss out on a promotion because you have fallen behind.

Now, expand this same rejection of accountability out to all areas of your life. What's the impact? Your girlfriend or wife becomes resentful because she can't say anything when you've forgotten to do something as she risks having you blow up or shut her out for days. Your friends don't bother to offer you advice or feedback because they know you aren't going to listen anyway, and slowly the number of people who can contribute to your life diminishes to zero. You feel "free" in the sense that no one can tell you what you're doing wrong, what you've missed or could improve, but you have also suffocated your ability to gain external perspective. Maybe you even take pride in this for a while and have let your ego become swollen by the notion that "I've made it on my own. I didn't need anyone's help."

Congratulations. *You officially cut everyone off from contributing to your life in a meaningful and valuable way.*

All sarcasm aside, men thrive when they are held accountable and find fulfillment in what they can contribute. Men specifically need to contribute. We *want* to contribute. So, when men gather and get together, it is natural for them to want to contribute to one another, often through the form of accountability, feedback, and direct support. The bond of brotherhood is deepened when we allow others to contribute to us. Receiving feedback, getting the opinions of men we trust and respect, and allowing others to share their perspectives allows us to see things we would otherwise miss.

Now, this doesn't mean you need to listen to or receive feedback from everyone. *Not all accountability is good or valuable.*

As I see it, there are three types of accountability:

1) Accountability we can and should ignore

2) Reciprocal accountability

3) Mentor accountability

First, *determining who you can and should be accountable with* is essential. For example, some random on the Internet who is trying to hold you accountable to their standards of what is virtuous, exceptional, or "morally good" may not be the best place to source your accountability. Social media has made it popular for strangers who have zero investment in your life to go online and attempt to hold you accountable to their views, opinions, and political and religious perspectives.

There are also people in your life who likely haven't earned a place at the table of accountability for various reasons. Perhaps they are selfish, manipulative, or dishonest. This doesn't mean you should ignore the insight of a friend simply because they don't have their life together; it simply means you should use discernment and really question their feedback.

Second is *reciprocal accountability*. This is the real bread and butter for men, but often the category men lack. These are the men in your life that you go to battle with. The men who are in your life and know your challenges, relationship, fears, strengths, goals, dreams, and darkness. They are the men you trust to act as external eyes, ears, and brains to spot the things about yourself and your life that you cannot possibly see. These are also the men you know deeply and trust implicitly. The accountability is reciprocal because it goes both ways: you are open to them giving you feedback, holding you accountable or calling you forward, and you are also willing to hold them accountable. These are the men you spend time with and for whom you make a concerted effort to deeply understand who it is *they say they want to become*. Once you understand this, you know what, where, and how to hold them accountable. Who does that man want to be as a father, partner, and business owner? What does he want financially, spiritually, and sexually within his relationship? From your vantage point, where does he fail to live up to that, and what would be beneficial for holding him accountable to stepping more fully into that role? If you don't have these men in your life, make this your main priority and focus immediately.

Lastly is *mentorship-based accountability*. This is a unidirectional form of accountability. Generally, this person isn't someone you are going to give feedback to, but rather someone who is directly mentoring you, holding you accountable, and guiding you. This form of accountability can be incredibly potent for you as a man because it requires that you trust deeply and surrender to another man's guidance. For some men, this will be the kind of accountability they resist even though it could be deeply healing to experience. I'm often asked how a man can find a mentor, and my answer is almost always the same—don't be afraid to pay for one. Who are the men you would actively *submit* to? Who are the men you would be honored to be led by? The men you would trust implicitly and, for a period, take their guidance as gospel? Find men you admire or respect and notice how dramatically your life shifts as a result of this mentorship.

To have a man hold you accountable is to know where you stand in that man's heart. To know that he gives enough of a shit to be uncomfortable in confronting you, challenging you, and holding you to your word. At the end of this book, you will find resources to develop friendship and brotherhood with men who will do exactly this—to develop an alliance of men all working together for the betterment of one another.

Mend your relationship to accountability at all costs and find freedom in the process.

CHAPTER 13

INTEGRATION

"The mind divides the world into a million pieces. The heart makes it whole."

STEPHEN LEVINE

WHEN I HOLD men's weekends and lead men through their inner work, I am often asked what it means to integrate something. The question usually sounds something like, "How can I integrate this part of me?" Or, "I hear people talking about the importance of integration—what does it really mean?" The word *integration* stems from the Latin nominative *integratio,* which means renewal and restoration. It also comes from the Latin *integrare,* which means to make whole or begin again. It implies that something will be returned to its most complete state, to be made sound, more healthy, more intact, or more complete.

If you've come this far in the book, you will surely have encountered a number of things that have been brought back into the wholeness of your being. You will have worked to face, confront, and accept things you've previously rejected, which has naturally led to integration.

For example, say you went through the chapter on anger and realized that you've been largely disconnected from your anger because of your past or a belief that it was dangerous. This means your anger had been abandoned to some degree and needed to be integrated back into your personality and identity. Rather than constantly trying to hide your anger, or disconnecting from it when you feel it, letting yourself experience and express your anger in a healthy way is the action of integrating it back into your personality.

In my time working with men, I've witnessed three types or categories of integration.

1) **Integrating what was lost or abandoned**

   Integrating what was lost or abandoned is similar to the example above about anger. This is when you rejected, neglected, or abandoned a part of yourself in order to fit in or survive. You may have lost or abandoned your assertiveness, compassion, discipline, or desire for intimacy for any number of reasons. Welcoming these parts back can bring up grief, anger, and pain from your past, but will always lead to a more complete version of who you are meant to be. During the course of this book, you've likely become aware of numerous behaviors, emotions, or skills that were abandoned. If you've been doing the work that coincides with this book, then you will have started the journey to integrate these parts back into your personality.

2) **Integrating what was never developed**

   I grew up with very little discipline. Because of this, discipline was not a natural skill or attribute I possessed. I didn't see the necessity for it, which was largely because I felt inferior when it came to discipline. For years I avoided it even as I saw the net-negative effect its absence was having on my life. I was scattered, disorganized, often late, and lacking in confidence because I felt out of control. Integrating discipline meant that I had to practice it. I had to develop and nurture discipline-oriented behaviors. This was not easy at first, but over time it became second nature. You will certainly have areas within your personality that were never developed—assertiveness, discipline, compassion, courage, expressing gratitude, asking for your needs: all of these can be developed, and as you develop them, you integrate them into your personality. There's no use for positive gain in shaming yourself or wishing you had started sooner. Start now. Develop these parts now. Look for what you never developed and aim to build it within yourself and your life.

3) **Integrating what was unknown**

This type of integration is a little more complex. To simplify, it is when we become aware of parts of ourselves, behaviors and actions, that previously were unknown to us. This happens when data or information from the unconscious mind comes into our conscious view, and we suddenly become aware of something that eluded us before. Maybe you have a dream where you solve a specific problem or you see yourself in someone else's behavior, which crystallizes a new kind of awareness about why you sabotage relationships or have behaved poorly with your wife. Integrating the unknown is a natural process you cannot force, but you can pay attention to it. If you look with curiosity at your dreams, start to notice yourself in others, and look at myths, symbols, and archetypes, unknown realizations will naturally occur. There will often be behavioral changes and shifts that accompany these realizations, but if you're paying attention, this will take care of itself or point you in the direction of the action you need to take.

Think about a part of yourself you've been trying to integrate—your anger, discipline, assertiveness, or compassion. Is this part something you lost, never developed, or has it always been unknown to you? Once you have the answer, ask yourself, *What would it look like for me to reclaim, develop, or know this part of myself? What actions, decisions, choices, conversations, and commitments can I make in order to integrate this part?*

Integration is both a conscious and unconscious process. It happens while you are working on it and deepens when you aren't looking.

Integration is a way of being—a practice and a way of orienting yourself in life. When you integrate lost behaviors, beliefs, or emotions, you naturally expand, and that expansion is a byproduct of integration. Growth is not a self-contained experience, but rather the result of having digested the much needed nutrients of integrating what we had lost, never developed, and didn't know about ourselves.

INTEGRATION EXERCISE

Let's explore what you have already started to integrate and get clear on what work still needs to be done.

1) Label and write out some of the behaviors, beliefs, and parts of yourself that you've already started to integrate through the process of this book (for example, skills, behaviors, and emotions).
2) What steps or actions have you taken to begin the process of integration? For example, if you are integrating assertiveness, what did you do to develop or allow it in? Having a tough conversation? Setting a boundary? Saying *no* when you'd normally back down?
3) What is it like to have integrated or started to integrate this, and what have the benefits been?
4) What are you still wanting to integrate that was lost or abandoned?
5) What are you still wanting to integrate that was never developed?
6) What would you need to commit to in order for this to happen?

INTEGRATION THROUGH FORGIVENESS: HOW DO I FORGIVE (MYSELF OR THEM)?

I am asked a version of this question every day: *How do I forgive myself or someone who hurt me?* I've found over the years that countless men feel stuck in some aspect of their integration and growth because they haven't been able to forgive someone, or themselves. This lack of forgiveness blocks us from being able to integrate the lessons from the betrayal or heal the pain, and is almost always an indicator that the behaviors, beliefs, and trust around this issue have yet to be resolved. Forgiveness can be either the block to integration or the sign that it's happening.

For months after I had betrayed myself, family, friends, and the women I dated, I asked myself the same question: How could I possibly be forgiven for the collection of betrayals I had amassed? It seemed insurmountable.

As I worked with my mentor, Bernard, the question began to emerge: "How do I forgive myself and others?" During one of our conversations, he asked me if I had been raised under any religion.

"Yes," I replied, "I was raised Roman Catholic. Why?"

"Do you remember the Lord's Prayer?" Bernard asked. "The one they say during every sermon."

"Yes, of course," I responded. "Why?"

"Well, what did it say about forgiveness?"

I thought for a few seconds and rattled off the verse, "'Forgive us our trespasses and forgive those who trespass against us.'"

"Do you know what that originally meant?" he asked.

"Not really, no," I said, wondering where he was going with this line of questioning.

"'Trespasses' meant debts. The original lines were *forgive us our debts, as we forgive our debtors.* They didn't mean money, although that may have sometimes been the case. The original statement was about wiping clean the debt that we feel is owed to us when we have been betrayed, trust has been broken, or we have been wronged in some way. Forgiveness is about getting clear about what you think you owe or are owed—emotionally, mentally, verbally, etc.—and either asking for it directly or wiping it clean entirely."

This is the case in most religions and spiritual practices. Suffering happens when there is a lack of forgiveness, and the act of forgiving is the path to liberation and integration.

When we have been betrayed or wronged by someone, we feel as though they owe us. When we have betrayed or wronged someone else, we feel as though we owe them.

We not only fall prey to the seductive belief that we are owed or owe someone, but we act from this place of indebtedness. It begins to shape our actions, decisions, behavior, and communication. We can act weak, needy, resentful, hateful, and justify all kinds of behavior because of the debt we feel.

Think about it for a moment: maybe you have let your partner down, cheated, or broken trust emotionally, sexually, or financially. You know you've hurt them and lost their trust, and so you feel like there is a debt of trust, connection, intimacy, communication, or love. You might find yourself scrambling to be on your best behavior, or to "make it up to them" and act from the place of "I owe you because I let you down." But what do you really owe them? This is the cloudy and vague nature of forgiveness—how can you tell if you've truly forgiven or been forgiven when you're operating from a deficit and the path to forgiveness is unknown?

Start by getting clear on what you feel is owed to you, and what you feel you owe the people you have hurt, broken trust with, and betrayed. This doesn't mean you deserve or are actually owed those things, but you'll understand specifically what you've been looking for in order for forgiveness to happen. Are you simply looking for an apology? Changed behavior? Time or attention? Are there certain words you need to hear? Are you looking for compassion and a deeper understanding of what the betrayal has caused you to experience or question? Or are you simply holding on because you don't want to face your own pain? Complete this sentence: *What I feel like they owe me is*_____________. Once you're clear on this, ask yourself whether this is something you really need for forgiveness to transpire, or if it's something you can relinquish fully. Is it a debt you can wipe clean?

But what about self-betrayal? How can you forgive yourself for betraying others and your own integrity? What do you owe you?

I remember sitting down one morning and journaling about this after my conversations with Bernard. "What do I owe myself?" I wrote, followed by, "How the hell should I know!? Maybe some self-respect? I owe myself a lot of things." And so, I started writing them all out—everything I owed myself. It was a long list. I realized that forgiving myself meant doing the things I had always avoided: giving myself compassion, developing discipline, giving myself room to fail and get it wrong, believing in myself, and building myself into a man I respected.

It meant I had to live in such a way that the forgiveness I was seeking from others and myself acted as the guide for my words, actions, and decisions.

Forgiveness, as I realized, isn't for the weak or feeble; it's for the bold and courageous. For the men looking to integrate the aspects of themselves that have seemed unreachable.

My challenge for you is to *let your life become the answer to the question of forgiveness.*

Let it shape you, sharpen you, and guide you on the path of releasing the emotional, relational, sexual, and psychological debts you have accumulated throughout your life, and watch as the man you are becomes the man you've always known you could be.

PART 4

LEGACY

CHAPTER 14

DEATH & LEGACY

"No legacy is so rich as honesty."

WILLIAM SHAKESPEARE

LEGACY IS THE ego's attempt at eternity. A way to live on past your physical form and attempt to cheat the finality of death. Traditionally *legacy* referred to the physical property you passed down to your descendants as a means of setting them up for a better future. Now it has become a siren song for men who have a deep fear that their life isn't meaningful, or at least not as meaningful as they say it is or would like it to be.

One day you'll die, and all that will remain is what you've built and what people remember about you. One day even that will fade. Realize that who you are now, in this moment and in every moment, is the legacy you will leave behind. It will be etched into the minds of the people you love and be decided by who you were, what you embodied, stood for, and taught.

A man who lives with betterment and expansion as his north star will naturally leave behind a legacy not because he needed to or had to for his life to mean something, but because he made his life mean something while living it.

Legacy is not an intention we should hold, but the side effect of a life lived meaningfully. The side effect of actualized purpose and potential.

Chase legacy, and you'll forever grasp at an illusion. Pursue purpose and meaning, and you'll leave behind something of substance.

The real question we all must ask ourselves when confronted by the question of legacy is, "Am I willing to see what I am truly capable of, *at all costs*?"

Are you willing to let go of the comforts you so desperately cling to and pursue your capabilities, without knowing the outcome? Can you delete the distractions off your phone, turn off the TV, put the junk food down, and charge forward? Are you willing to work tirelessly and allow yourself to be forged into being by the adventures, failures, experiences, and obstacles that arise when living your purpose? If so, then press forward and be relentless in bettering yourself.

Don't get caught fixating on your future and what you might miss out on while living the life you have built now and the man you are in this moment. Be fully present and without distraction for your children as often as you can manage. Sit with your wife, friends, and family and look them in the eyes while you listen to their problems. Give what you can, when you can, to the absolute fullest of your capacity, and what you stand for as a man will be imprinted on all those you crossed paths with.

But above all, let your legacy and your life be an honest one.

Practice dying before you die. Let the stagnant beliefs, relationships, and activities in your life end. Most men do not fear the end or termination of something but the grief and uncertainty that comes with it. What we really fear is the unknown that lingers at the precipice just beyond the threshold of an end, limitation, or termination. Death, or any ending for that matter, is the pure, condensed, one-hundred-proof version of the unknown.

But this is the practice, my friend. It is something you must witness in your daily life. The ending of a conversation that will never happen again or a belief that no longer serves you. The death of a relationship, parent, career, who you thought your partner was, and the death of your constant expectations. All of it must be faced, felt, and welcomed.

The hidden truth about your personal development, or personal growth, is that it is equally a practice in personal death. It is a practice of honoring the psychospiritual aspects of you that are shedding and constantly dying. What makes growth challenging is often the white-knuckled grip we have on the thing we most need to let go of and let die.

As you grow and develop new beliefs, habits, and relationships, the old ones inevitably fade and die away. Betterment is as much about death as it is about growth or life. And this is the real challenge for most. Often, our unwillingness to embrace an ending, a limitation, or a death is the very thing holding us back.

A few years ago, I started a practice of meditating daily on my own death. I'd had a number of near-death experiences—some because of my own stupidity, some because of the stupidity of others, and some because of circumstances I still can't explain. After one such event, I got curious about what it would look like to integrate death into my life. I had read a lot about *memento mori*, the ancient practice of remembering death, or that you will die, but hadn't instituted any rituals to bring this practice into my life.

One morning, out of pure curiosity, I calculated a rough estimate of how many days I had left to live. I took the average lifespan for a man living in North America (80), subtracted my age (34), and multiplied that number by the number of days in a year . . .

16,790 days.

16,790 left to live.

Maybe a few more or a few less.

Roughly 402,960 hours to breathe, enjoy, explore, and experience life in this human form. This is, of course, if I am fortunate enough to last that long.

It was an odd number to see and an even stranger thing to feel in my gut. I wondered for a while what I should make of the number. 16,790. Was that it? Didn't seem like a lot. I'd had more debt on my credit card at one point in my life than the days left to live, which was admittedly a concerning thought.

I remember sitting at my desk trying to determine what I was supposed to do with this number and how it related to death—or should I say my life? It brought up a lot of questions about how I wanted to spend each day and what I wanted my life to mean. What did I want to do? Where did I want to travel? What did I want to build? I didn't know where to begin, so I committed to a morning protocol of counting down the days of my life.

Each morning for the next several months, I woke up, subtracted a day from my life, and wrote about what it was like knowing that my life was coming to an end. I started to get a real sense of how minor some of the problems in my life really were and how futile it was to hold onto regrets. We as men can get trapped in our quest for eternity and infinite understanding, always needing to have certainty, the answer, and our desire to have the complex entanglements of life's problems unwrapped neatly and solved before our eyes. But this is rarely the case.

I found an odd sense of calm mixed with a new quality of urgency begin to emerge. A renewed sense of focus and clarity came in and I was forced to confront the fear I had around death. I was, up until that point, convinced that I wasn't afraid to die, but after doing this practice I had come to realize that it was life I was afraid of. Life was the real threat. It was immediate and in my face. It brought all kinds of hardship, loss, grief, and confusion. But slowly, death informed how I lived.

For this reason, we must practice witnessing death. Acknowledging where we have reached the end, hit a limit, and allowing ourselves grace to honor the deaths that take place all around us. To embrace each moment not because it might be our last, but because it genuinely is the last moment of its kind.

Practice letting go. Practice surrendering the mind. Practice letting your mind find stillness in a more diffused, dispersed way of being. Practice letting go of your attachment to anything and everything, evaporating into nothing. Face the unnerving fear that accompanies death as often as you can and find stillness in its presence.

As you close the final chapter to this book, ask yourself what about you has died or is dying away as a result of your work. What story, belief, or behavior is dying because you have committed yourself to the work of bettering yourself as a man? Whatever it is, honor it, accept it, and release it just as I honor you, accept you, and release you with the deepest gratitude and respect for taking the steps to grow deeper into who you are as a man.

QUESTIONS TO ANSWER ▸ TRUTHS TO UNCOVER

To me death is . . .

The role death has played in my life is . . .

If I died tomorrow, the legacy I'd leave behind is . . .

What I've learned about myself through this work is . . .

What I'm letting die away is . . .

The one thing I've begun to implement is . . .

What I'm taking with me is . . .

I want to celebrate myself for . . .

What I've learned about my shadow is . . .

What I have begun to cultivate and integrate is . . .

What I'm committed to working on moving forward is . . .

EPILOGUE

BUILDING AN ALLIANCE OF MEN

AN *ALLIANCE* IS defined as *a union or association formed for mutual benefit.* I built the ManTalks Alliance for this sole purpose—to be a mutual benefit for all the men who are willing to engage in the direct, open, and growth-oriented conversations.

My challenge for you is to develop your own alliance, whether with the men already in your life or through the Alliance that we have already built with men from around the world.

This section will share the critical pieces to developing your own alliance.

BUILD YOUR BROTHERHOOD

I am often asked by men who are beginning to develop themselves how they can find new male friendships that will support them.

My answer is simple: *Go where the man you want to be would spend time and join groups of men building themselves in the ways you are committed to.*

Maybe that man is at the gym, in a business mastermind, in a group like the ManTalks Alliance, or at a men's weekend. Perhaps he is building something you can contribute to or learn from. It might be a specific workshop, retreat, business, or financial forum.

Be direct about your intentions. For example, the ManTalks Alliance is intended to provide a place where you can surround yourself with like-minded men who are doing inner work and bettering themselves as fathers, husbands, and leaders. Maybe your intention is to develop more meaningful and depth-oriented relationships with the men in your life, or at the very least to stop lying and tell the truth with the men you are already friends with. See if they are willing to engage with you in this intention.

Next, learn how to challenge the men you surround yourself with and be challenged by them.

CHALLENGE OVER COMPETITION

Restore your masculine relationships by moving from competition-based relationships to challenge-oriented relationships. Many men are surrounded by men they subtly feel in competition with. They share stories about their sexual conquests or how much money they're making but fail to challenge one another in meaningful, generative ways. To be clear, competition isn't a bad thing and certainly has a place within your male relationships.

Be willing to have your own bullshit reflected back at you in the form of the feedback and confrontation you've likely been avoiding in your life.

CALLING MEN FORWARD

Male relationships thrive on accountability and die without it. A relationship with a man without accountability is more of an acquaintanceship than an actual friendship. Our lack of accountability or willingness to call a man forward into a greater version of himself sends the signal that we lack interest in his life. It is for this very reason that so many men feel alone or lack real friendship. If you are one of these men, you likely have male friends; you just don't have friends who have the balls to confront you when you need it the most. And the same goes for you: you have likely failed the men in your life by witnessing their struggles firsthand and not calling them forward into a better version of themselves.

Calling a man forward is about them, not you. When you "call someone out," it's about you and your ego. It's about how you "showed them" or "put them in their place." This, however, is not helpful with friends and generally doesn't do anything to create any real progress. But it feels good in the moment.

Calling a man forward is all about him. It's about *who he has said he wants to be.* It's about knowing a man well enough to see the kind of father, husband, leader, entrepreneur he wants to be and holding him to that vision.

You might notice that a close friend has been drinking more than usual after saying they wanted to cut back and prioritize their health. Calling him forward in this example means confronting him about the commitment he made and asking him why he has been doing the opposite of what he said he would do. It might sound something like this: "Last week, you made a commitment to cut back on drinking, but you're drinking more than usual this week. How come?"

Or, if you have a shared understanding of calling one another forward, it might sound like this:

"Hey man, I'm going to call you forward. Last week you committed to cutting back on drinking, but I've noticed you've been drinking more than normal. What happened to your commitment, and are you willing to clean it up?"

Create a culture within your male relationships of calling one another forward. Forward into the man you want to be, the man you believe you are capable of becoming, and the man you know will leave his mark on the world.

As the African proverb says, "If you want to go fast, go alone. If you want to go far, go together." Find men you can go far with, and the speed will surpass what you could do alone.

#MANITFORWARD

The code of Man It Forward is simple: be willing to take direct and honest action toward lifting the men around you. This might mean starting a group that meets monthly and uses the principles in this book (or any book) as a discussion point. It might mean going out of your way to support a man who has recently gone through a divorce or breakup, organizing an event for a man who is entering into fatherhood, or finding ways to add value to something a man is building (his relationship, business, career, education, home, etc.). Man It Forward means taking the lessons, compassion, and strength you've acquired through your development and passing it on. It means taking the wisdom, mentorship, and opportunities you've been given and passing them on to those you want to invest in.

Man It Forward can include small or large actions. Here are a few you can execute in your daily or weekly life:

— Check in on a man who would usually not ask for support.

— Gift a man a resource that will help him better himself in an area he wants to develop.

— Send a book, podcast, or program that has helped you to a man who you know would benefit from it.

— Take the initiative of planning a trip or gathering for the men closest to you.

What a man gives to you or has given to you, Man It Forward to another man in your life. Let a part of your legacy be the contribution you make to the men in your life. When you are of service to other men, you are of service to all.

REFERENCES

Carl Jung, *Man and His Symbols* (New York: Doubleday, 1964).

Stephen Porges, *The Polyvagal Theory: Neurophysiological Foundations of Emotions, Attachment, Communication, and Self-Regulation* (New York: W.W. Norton, 2011).

Brené Brown, *Daring Greatly: How the Courage to Be Vulnerable Transforms the Way We Live, Love, Parent, and Lead* (New York: Gotham, 2012).

Robert E. Pyke, "Sexual Performance Anxiety," *Sexual Medicine Reviews* 8, no. 2 (April 2020): 183–190, pubmed.ncbi.nlm.nih.gov/31447414/.

Christopher Ingraham, "The Share of Americans Not Having Sex Has Reached a Record High," *The Washington Post*, March 29, 2019, washingtonpost.com/business/2019/03/29/share-americans-not-having-sex-has-reached-record-high/.

Richard Fry, "For First Time in Modern Era, Living With Parents Edges Out Other Living Arrangements for 18- to 34-Year-Olds," Pew Research Center, May 24, 2016, pewresearch.org/social-trends/2016/05/24/for-first-time-in-modern-era-living-with-parents-edges-out-other-living-arrangements-for-18-to-34-year-olds/.

Sara Hunter Murray, "I Want You to Want Me: A Qualitative Analysis of Heterosexual Men's Desire to Feel Desired in Intimate Relationships,"

Journal of Sex & Marital Therapy 47, no. 5 (2021): 419–434, tandfonline.com/doi/abs/10.1080/0092623X.2021.1888830.

Simone Kühn, "Brain Structure and Functional Connectivity Associated With Pornography Consumption: The Brain on Porn," *JAMA Psychiatry* 71, no. 7 (2014): 827–834, jamanetwork.com/journals/jamapsychiatry/fullarticle/1874574.

Nathaniel M. Lambert et al., "A Love That Doesn't Last: Pornography Consumption and Weakened Commitment to One's Romantic Partner," *Journal of Social and Clinical Psychology* 31, no. 4, 410–438, doi.org/10.1521/jscp.2012.31.4.410.

Chyng Sun, "Pornography and the Male Sexual Script: An Analysis of Consumption and Sexual Relations," *Archives of Sexual Behavior* 45, no. 4 (2016): 983–994, doi.org/10.1007/s10508-014-0391-2.

ABOUT THE AUTHOR

CONNOR BEATON is the founder of ManTalks, an international organization focused on men's wellness, success, and fulfillment. He is a coach, facilitator, teacher, podcast host, and speaker helping men from all over the world find purpose, healthy love, a joy-filled life, and fulfilling sexual connection. His teachings draw from an in-depth apprenticeship in Jungian psychology, gestalt, cognitive behavioral therapy, and both Buddhist and Taoist traditions.

Connor has a no-BS approach coupled with compassionate understanding of our own human limitations. He has coached thousands of men through private coaching, group work, workshops, retreats, and masterminds, and he has shared the stage with world-class speakers like Gary Vaynerchuk, Lewis Howes, Danielle LaPorte, and many more.

For more, visit mantalks.com.

ABOUT SOUNDS TRUE

SOUNDS TRUE is a multimedia publisher whose mission is to inspire and support personal transformation and spiritual awakening. Founded in 1985 and located in Boulder, Colorado, we work with many of the leading spiritual teachers, thinkers, healers, and visionary artists of our time. We strive with every title to preserve the essential "living wisdom" of the author or artist. It is our goal to create products that not only provide information to a reader or listener but also embody the quality of a wisdom transmission.

For those seeking genuine transformation, Sounds True is your trusted partner. At SoundsTrue.com you will find a wealth of free resources to support your journey, including exclusive weekly audio interviews, free downloads, interactive learning tools, and other special savings on all our titles.

To learn more, please visit SoundsTrue.com/freegifts or call us toll-free at 800.333.9185.